OPENING GOLIATH

Danger and Discovery in Caving

OPENING GOLIATH

CARY J. GRIFFITH

BOREALIS
BOOKS

Borealis Books is an imprint of the
Minnesota Historical Society Press.
www.borealisbooks.org

© 2009 by Cary J. Griffith. All rights re-
served. No part of this book may be used
or reproduced in any manner whatsoever
without written permission except in the
case of brief quotations embodied in crit-
ical articles and reviews. For information,
write to Borealis Books, 345 Kellogg Blvd.
W., St. Paul, MN 55102-1906.

The Minnesota Historical Society Press
is a member of the Association of American University Presses.

Manufactured in the
United States of America

10 9 8 7 6 5 4 3 2 1

∞ The paper used in this publication
meets the minimum requirements of the
American National Standard for Information Sciences—Permanence for Printed
Library Materials, ANSI Z39.48-1984.

International Standard Book Number
ISBN 13: 978-0-87351-649-5
ISBN 10: 0-87351-649-4

Library of Congress
Cataloging-in-Publication Data

Griffith, Cary J.
Opening goliath : danger and discovery
in caving / Cary J. Griffith.
      p.   cm.
      Includes bibliographical references.
      ISBN-13: 978-0-87351-649-5
      (cloth : alk. paper)
      ISBN-10: 0-87351-649-4
      (cloth : alk. paper)
      1. Caving.
      I. Title.
GV200.62.G75 2009
796.52′5—dc22   2009001715

Opening Goliath was designed by Will
Powers at the Minnesota Historical Soci-
ety Press, set in Bulmer and Franklin
Gothic type by Judy Gilats at Peregrine
Graphic Services, St. Paul, and printed by
Sheridan Books, Ann Arbor.

For Anna. I am blessed with a partner who shares my love of wild places.

And for Nick, Noah, and Jess, who like a good story and on more than one occasion have patiently listened to the old man tell one.

OPENING GOLIATH

AUTHOR'S NOTE

When I started writing this book, I had visited a wild cave only once. We entered through a two-foot hole that bellied out beneath a limestone slab with fourteen inches of crawl space. I hustled to the other side, my heart ringing in my ears. We spent two hours climbing through that wild cave, where I saw incredible formations and ultimately reached a place called Enigma Pit: a deep hole where the sides of the cave fell away and disappeared into a craggy, dripping, black crevasse.

Opening Goliath, a book in three parts, is about cave exploration, danger, politics, science, discovery, subterranean wonder, and the unknown. Part One describes a near-death cave-diving attempt to find the way into an elusive cave frontier that probably runs for thirty miles near the Minnesota-Iowa border. It also introduces readers to some of the bizarre history and mystery of the man-made caves along the West Side bluffs in St. Paul.

Part Two takes place on a Tuesday afternoon in April 2004, when five high school kids decide to explore one of St. Paul's man-made caves. The tragic events that day begin to explain the differences between man-made and wild caves, the methods of inexperienced and experienced cavers, and the reasons government organizations like the City of St. Paul and the Minnesota Department of Natural Resources strive to prevent or control access to our underground resources.

Part Three uses the discovery and exploration of Goliath's Cave, a large wild cave in southern Minnesota's karst region, as a stage. It explores our fascination with unknown places, helping to show why some of us will literally risk our lives to go where no one else has ever set foot. Goliath's Cave is also the place where competing governmental, scientific, public, and private interests converge, grappling with how best to enter, explore, and use our underground resources—in a way that will ensure they are preserved for future generations.

OPENING GOLIATH

PART ONE

Dangerous Explorations

Southeastern Minnesota karst region, 2001,
& St. Paul, 2004

1
Doorway to the Odessa
Odessa Spring, near Granger, Minnesota
Sunday, April 29, 2001

John Ackerman steps into the water-filled passageway fins first. His pulse races, and a wave of anxiety spreads across his body until it settles in his head. His head tells him he must be crazy. Many times in his forty-seven years, Ackerman has pushed through underworld passages—some so narrow he had to strip to his waist in wet, almost freezing conditions to get to the other side. At five feet eleven inches, 160 pounds, with a gymnast's thin, muscular body, he is a seasoned cave explorer. But cave *diving* is the most dangerous recreational sport in the world, and this is only his third dive—and the third time he has entered this passage. He feels certain that one of the largest undiscovered cave systems in the Upper Midwest is hidden just beyond this watery entrance. And for that he is willing to risk what common sense tells him may very well be a fool's errand, or the most dangerous afternoon of his life.

Nature has taken eons to carve this rough column out of rock. The persistent force of slightly acidic water has acted like a drill bit on the soft limestone substrate. But the chute, angling down in an almost vertical shaft, is anything but regular. Over millennia, the water flow loosened sedimentary rock and left jagged, irregular walls pockmarked with phantom holes that lead into sucker passageways. Those dead-end holes can add to the underwater confusion. What's more, his diving partner, Mark Henderson, an experienced Florida cave diver, has already descended into the chute, worked his way toward its bottom, and clouded the waters. Within minutes Henderson resurfaced. He stuck his masked head above the water, took the regulator out of his mouth, and said, "It's blocked."

"Blocked?"

"Down near the bottom. Must have been a fresh rock fall since last week."

"I'm going to have a look," Ackerman said.

"Suit yourself," Henderson said, and moved out of the chute.

Henderson had anchored their dive reel at the bottom in a copse of rock, because he knows John Ackerman. He suspected the monomaniacal caver would want to follow their thick nylon descent rope into the water and see for himself. Or *feel* for himself, given that Henderson's movement through the water riled it to an opaque brown. If Ackerman can find a way around the blockage, he will want to take up the anchored reel and continue probing the underwater cave.

Before Henderson made his first descent, the two men had argued about gear. Henderson wanted Ackerman to use a harness plate to affix the large air tank to his back. Ackerman was against it. He's had little experience cave diving, but plenty in Minnesota's caves. He'll be squeezing through places too small for his body with a tank strapped to his back. And with the tank on his back, the regulator hose and turn-off valves would be somewhere behind his neck. In blackout conditions, if there were problems, tracing the proper hose to the proper valve would be impossible. Ackerman was adamant about not wearing the back plate—far better to have a small makeshift harness he can use to pull the tank behind him or move it to his side. Henderson acquiesced, but he told Ackerman he had to wear the fins. Ackerman wanted no part of the fins because he thought they were unwieldy and unnecessary and would only further cloud the water. But since he'd won the battle over the back plate, he deferred to Henderson's greater cave-diving experience. Besides, when they had practiced in Henderson's dark apartment pool, Ackerman had learned how to reach neutral buoyancy—that place of underwater weightlessness in which you neither rise nor sink. Henderson assured him if he was able to maintain neutral buoyancy and move with his diving fins, he might be able to avoid clouding the water.

Henderson's descent and return has turned the water a muddy tan—the color of the limestone cliff face under which this spring boils out of the ground.

Ackerman tries not to think about the blackout conditions. He has focused on every step of preparation: the drive down to the remote Minnesota border region, hauling their tanks fifty yards through the woods to the limestone cliff face, pulling on his seven-mil wet suit, cleaning his mask. Now, he envisions another column, rising not far from the few brief feet they have already explored into an underground cavern, this one open and air filled. It is the gateway to the Odessa Spring system, a series of interconnected caves that some geologists and cavers estimate contains over thirty miles of unexplored openings and passages. Ackerman is determined to find the entry point that will open up the massive subsurface wilderness of waterfalls, fossils, and ancient stone formations.

On the embankment five feet above the two men, Amos Yoder, the Amish man who owns the land, looks on. His broad-brimmed hat and faded homespun cut a wide shadow in the afternoon light. Next to Yoder, Henderson's wife snaps pictures of the two men standing in the ditch of murky water. Beside her is Dave Gerboth, another longtime caver who has explored this region with Ackerman since the start of their effort to find the doorway into the Odessa. Gerboth holds the end of the heavy nylon cord. If he feels three tugs on the rope, Ackerman is in trouble. At that point he can pull, or send Henderson into the water for rescue.

Ackerman rests his large, fluorescent green air tank on the bank and pushes on the regulator's diaphragm. Air bursts through the opening, punctuating the quiet of remote woods. Then he inserts the mouthpiece and breathes, making sure the apparatus is operational.

The late April afternoon is sunny and bright, and the temperature has climbed above 60 degrees. But the outflow from this wide underground spring is 16 degrees above freezing. Through his wet suit he can feel the temperature envelop his feet, then calves, knees, thighs—it is the kind of cold that can kill an ill-equipped man in less than five minutes. Now it seeps into the small edges of his suit, sends a brief cold rush into the thin layer between his skin and the wet suit wall. His body heat quickly warms the cold water to 98.6 degrees, and suddenly he can breathe again. Before he descends, he works through one last mental checklist of equipment preparations and his plan of attack.

"Ready?" Henderson asks.

Ackerman looks up, the dive mask perched on top of his hooded forehead. He remembers the silvery edge of a line-cutting knife he watched Henderson tuck into his dive belt. He knows you can never be too careful. "Maybe I should borrow your knife?"

Henderson pulls it out and hands it over.

The knife, designed for working blind underwater, has a blade less than two inches long with a hooked edge and a razor-sharp crook. John attaches the two-inch strap with its snug sheath to one of his harness straps. "Thanks," he says. "Ready."

Finally, Ackerman lowers his face mask and begins working his way backward into the earthen-colored brew, his pulse kicking up another notch. His head drops beneath the surface, and he is immersed in cold. He pauses, checking his apparatus, holding the fluorescent green tank above him. Once underwater his head is filled with the sound of his inhaled breath. Then his exhale rises in a burst of bubbles.

Only inches beneath the sunny surface the world turns cloudy, then muddy, then entirely dark. Attached to his wrist with a nylon lanyard hangs a high-powered underwater flashlight, but it is worthless in this kind of water. His twelve-pound weight belt helps him sink. But he needs to drop slowly and carefully through the seventeen-foot shaft—in places less than three feet wide—like a blind man descending into a rough earthen well.

* * *

John Ackerman begins his descent into the Odessa Spring. Courtesy John Ackerman

Every year the National Speleological Society publishes shorthand accounts of cave explorations gone awry. In a special section for *Cave Diving Accidents and Incidents,* the statistics underscore the danger. For the year 2000 the report noted ten cave-diving fatalities. The causes included inadequate equipment, siltation, poor training, bad air in a gas pocket, no guidelines, and deep diving on too little air.

Ackerman has read these records and also studied the manuals. The National Speleological Society's *Cave Diving Manual* (1998), which contains practical information, including sections on dive planning, basic equipment, underwater cave fauna, and hypothermia, even has a segment called *psychological aspects.* Ackerman's dive today is dangerous, but he has a clear plan, the right equipment, and experience—at least with Minnesota's caves. A paragraph in the manual's psychology section made him smile, though, wondering if the text's author played Dungeons and Dragons, or maybe was a Tolkien fan. It referred to the "crescendo of events" and "having to slay your dragon."

> Remember the cascade of events. If you are in a spot where there is no margin for error, you will execute a flawless dive if you slow down and remain in charge of your head. The Dragon lives at the base of your skull. When you wake him, you will first feel his fiery breath reaching upward under your hair between your ears. If you fail to slay your Dragon, he will slay you.

The "cascade of events" resonates. Over almost two decades of caving Ackerman has found himself in many tight spots. But he's never met the dragon. He reminds himself to pay attention—maybe he can add dragon slayer to his long list of caving accomplishments.

He brings the tank down after him, breathing steadily.

* * *

During his twenties and early thirties, Ackerman focused on building up his furniture restoration business, Ackerman's Furniture Service, which now has twelve employees and a state-of-the-art restoration facility. The business thrived, providing him with the financial resources to pursue his passion. Over the last decade he has increasingly spent his spare time in the pursuit of discovering and opening up virgin cave. He has owned Spring Valley Caverns, now the second-longest cave in the state, since 1989. That year he also created the Minnesota Karst Preserve and began adding more cave properties to his holdings, often with controversy. Many people do not agree with his methods of creating new entryways into caves.

But no matter, Ackerman now thinks. Truth is, he feels completely caught up in this latest effort to locate the entrance to the Odessa system. He feels certain today he is knocking on the door.

It has been less than a year since he and Dave Gerboth discovered this small opening in the remote cliff face near the town of Granger on the Iowa border. Southeast Minnesota is known for its karst topography. Over four hundred million years ago in the Ordovician Period, when this area was covered with a great sea, layers and layers of shell debris were deposited and then compressed into limestone as other layers of sedimentary rock were deposited. Although the area was glaciated early in the last Ice Age, it missed the later stages that ground the rest of the state flat. Erosion has had more than a million years here to remove glacial drift and expose the limestone bedrock. Eons of snowmelt and rainfall, carrying minute concentrations of carbonic acid, have bored into and under the limestone, creating caves throughout this karst region.

Now the rolling terrain holds dairy farms—and some of the largest undiscovered and unexplored cave systems in the United States.

Ackerman is new to scuba diving. Less than two months earlier he finished his classroom training and did his open water certification in a Florida resort, where the waters were warm, clear, and sparkling. He'd acquired his diver's license so he could drop into this darkened shaft. His heartbeat rises in his chest. His breathing is measured but rapid. He focuses on his descent.

Last week the spring runoff swelled this escaping water to a rushing fountain. He managed to get down into the watery column, but the rush of water almost tore the regulator out of his mouth. This week the water rises more slowly, and he moves down the shaft, feeling for the place where Henderson claims the bottom has been blocked.

Ackerman and Henderson have been back to this site three times, and on each dive they've been able to push a few feet farther. First they managed to find their way to the bottom of this seventeen-foot chute. There you place your feet onto a flat slab of limestone and make a 180-degree turn into a cloudy, underwater room. But the first time Ackerman dove it, the water was so dirty he could only venture along a stretch of winding tunnel by hand. And then last Sunday, when both of them were fifteen feet along the subterranean passage, Henderson's dive reel froze. This cylindrical wheel, wrapped with one-eighth-inch nylon cord, is their lifeline to the surface. While they move forward, it plays out behind them, pulling off the reel inches at a time. The wheel assembly stopped turning.

They struggled in the murky water, trying to fix it. But

their flashlights were useless, and working with hands sheathed in diving gloves was like picking up dimes wearing mittens. And of course they could not take off their gloves. After one or two minutes in 48-degree water, bare hands go numb and the joints start to slow and seize up, causing virtual paralysis. They began to run out of oxygen and had to surface.

Over the subsequent week, Henderson realized the dive reel's housing assembly was missing two bolts. He repaired it and added small knots in the nylon cord to measure off ten-foot increments. And today he anchored it near the pit's bottom, at the end of their descent rope, just in case he was wrong about the pit's blockage and Ackerman could pick up the reel and continue exploring.

Cave-diving exploration involves a process referred to as *moving the reel forward.* If Ackerman can find the place where Henderson anchored the dive reel and discover a way around the obstruction, he can play out the nylon cord. As he moves, the reel will map his trail through the unexplored passages. He will push as far as he can and then anchor the dive reel in place. He can follow the cord out to the surface. And the next time they enter the underwater world, they can move quickly along the line to the dive reel and push farther ahead. That is, *if* John Ackerman doesn't first discover the gateway to the Odessa.

Now Ackerman approaches the dark bottom of the pit, feeling carefully around the obstruction for the dive reel and picking it up. He finds another hole to one side, large enough to enter. Sure enough, just a few feet farther he is through what Henderson mistook for blockage, entering the last section of chute bottom. It seems as though the water has cleared. He thinks he might be able to see more than a couple inches of dark murkiness, and he switches on his light.

Less than a foot from his face his beam illuminates the rock wall. The current flows up, and because Henderson didn't make it to the bottom, this section is clear. Under the light the water glistens like crystal.

Ackerman carefully twists, making his 180-degree rotation, keeping his flashlight beam in front of him. He holds the dive reel in his other hand, playing out nylon cord. And then he looks up and follows his beam's light into the underwater cave and he is . . . mesmerized.

He peers into a room ten feet square with clearly visible walls and a ceiling that reaches into darkness. Boulders and jagged rocks protrude from two side walls cut out of limestone. He has been here before, but the water has never been so clear. The room and its walls are shimmering blue green and beautiful, like the beckoning turquoise of a summer swimming pool, sparkling in the curious cut of his light. Another large opening yawns across the room. He is going to find his doorway.

He pauses with his feet on the solid limestone floor long enough to take in the miracle of this underwater room. He inhales, thinking this space is like a vestibule, a threshold to a new world. Down here there is only the sound of his breathing, like Darth Vader's slow inhale and exhale. And his bubbles. He can hear them rise above him and disappear up the chute.

He turns and looks up the chute, aiming his beam into the dark tunnel. The silt has been settling for thousands of years, covering everything with a half-inch blanket of dust. Before last week, this stretch of territory had never been touched. Other than spring runoff and the occasional summer rainstorms, the chamber maintains a steady flow of water. There has never been anything else to stir the silt and raise it off the flowage bottom and underwater walls.

When he shines his light above him, his beam disappears into the thick black cloud of the column. He holds the diving reel in his right hand and sees the white cord disappear into the murk. Even if this entire room becomes mired and black, Ackerman will be able to use the thin nylon cord to retrace his passage through this underwater world—and to exit the black chute.

He pushes across the room, trying to move forward without creating too much current. After the narrow chute, the room appears cavernous. Ackerman moves toward the tunnel, breathing steadily, careful to maintain his buoyancy. Even though his fins are useful in this open area, he still wishes he had left them on the surface. The small space toward which he moves is narrowing and twisting, and in less than five more feet he is in it. One easy kick lifts the ancient silt from the bottom, and the room fills in behind him, as impenetrable as steeped black tea.

He keeps moving. He will not enter a passage he cannot see, but if he has clear visibility—as he does here, now—he can examine the passage. He can memorize its walls, overall size and shape, any obstructions or phantom holes he must avoid. Once he frames a passage in his mind, he can find his way back through it, even though this one bends down, then up, makes one turn, then another.

He drags the dive reel beside him, careful to keep the unwinding rope clear of his equipment. His tank rests in its makeshift harness on his other side. The tunnel narrows and twists down; like the seventeen-foot vertical shaft, its sides are jagged, and occasionally he has to work around large pieces of stone. But he keeps moving, well beyond the farthest point they reached the week before. He knows if he can just keep moving, the tunnel will eventually rise upward. But in these tight quarters, moving slowly, clouding the water is inevitable.

Now Ackerman takes fifteen minutes to push another fifty feet, bumping and pulling along the twisting tunnel, waiting for its angled rise or the appearance of a yawning dark shaft above him. But after he passes through seventy-five, maybe eighty feet of unexplored tunnel, the silty water finally catches up with him. The cloud follows him into a six-foot-wide space. Ahead he can see more tunnel. There is a large flat boulder to his left. If he can anchor the dive reel on that stone shelf, he can move to the other side of the tunnel, carefully turn around, recover his line, and follow the eighth-inch nylon cord through the twisting passage, through the vestibule, and up into the chute that will return him to safety. It is time to return to the surface.

Moments before this small horizontal room disappears in a thick black cloud, he anchors his dive reel on the stone shelf. And then everything goes dark. The silt-out is complete, and he begins moving to the other side of the chamber, stretching out his right hand to feel for the wall. He hugs the wall opposite the dive reel so when he makes his small, careful turn, no part of his equipment will become entangled in the knotted line.

He turns, very carefully, abiding by the room size and his detailed memory of the small passage. Though he cannot see which way is up or down, left or right, he can feel the walls. If he moves carefully he should be able to complete his turn, re cover the line, and follow it through darkness to safety.

He guesses he has been under for more than fifteen minutes. He should still have plenty of air. Cave divers need to mind their oxygen and time. Ackerman entered this cave without a pressure gauge to tell him exactly how much air he has left. Not that he would be able to read it in this dark water. From his limited diving experience, he knows he doesn't use much oxygen. The eighty-cubic-foot diving tank tucked in the harness to his side, riding up a little on his back, should give him up to an hour of breathing time, almost triple what he needs. By the time he reaches the surface, if everything goes as planned, he should have at least a half hour to spare.

He turns toward his right, ready to follow the dive reel line to the cave's exit. But then he feels a tug at his left foot. At first he is startled and jerks his foot. The tug tightens, and in one quick moment he realizes his left fin has somehow become entangled in the diving reel cord.

No problem, he thinks. He begins to reach down with his left hand and by muffled feel free the cord around his fin. But it is difficult to feel a one-eighth-inch cord through seven-mil diving gloves. He begins moving his hand back, thinking he might try another maneuver. But now the nylon lanyard holding the flashlight to his left wrist tightens. As he tries to bring his left hand away from his left fin, the lanyard pulls at him. With a sunken feeling and a small edge of panic, he realizes his flashlight has become entangled with his foot and the line.

"Damn those fins!" he thinks, remembering he didn't want them.

With his right hand he reaches up to recover the diving reel, thinking he will use it to feed down the length of line and untangle himself.

But the reel is gone.

He feels for it along the flat shelf, trying to grab it with his heavy gloves. He is certain he is feeling along the ledge where only moments earlier he anchored it. But it's gone! His heart hammers in its bone cage. He feels again for the cord, picks up what he thinks is the line and, yes, there is a small knot in the cord where just this week Henderson tied it. And it eases his panic, just a little, to know he is at least gripping the anchored line.

He struggles to understand the sudden disappearance of the dive reel. There must have been something behind the shelf. Maybe a back edge to the shelf, a cavity behind it?

In fact, there is a precipice just the other side of the flat stone, a deep hole he could not see. When he placed the dive reel on its edge, the cloud of silt began to fill in around it, and John Ackerman could not see the reel drop into an abyss, feeding out line as it fell.

He has the cord in his right hand, but his left is still caught up with his fin, and he is bent with his right hand stretched, holding the cord. He decides he'll pull out more cord, pull it out until the diving reel catches and then he can snap the nylon cord, untangle himself, and follow the line to safety.

He struggles to focus. His heart hammers and his breathing ratchets up another notch, because in this kind of wilderness small mistakes can easily snowball, building on each other until an avalanche drops its unexpected weight on top of you. Ackerman remembers the ten cave divers who died just last year.

Don't, he thinks. Don't recollect it. Don't go there. Focus.

He pauses, breathing, trying to calm himself. And then he starts pulling on the cord, pulling it off the reel. He pulls and pulls and pulls, and pretty soon there is a loose floating web of nylon cord in the black space around him. But he does not see the web. He keeps pulling. Eventually the end of the line goes taut, and Ackerman braces himself, taking firm hold of the line, starting to pull it, expecting it to snap. He pulls hard, trying to break it. But eighth-inch nylon cord is strong—it has a tensile strength of three hundred pounds—and is virtually impossible to snap one-handed in weightless conditions.

Ackerman turns hard, trying to free himself from the web of line. And then he feels something catching on his back, something tight. His movement sends a burst of air escaping from his tank. He hears it in the darkness: the change in air-flow, the sudden accelerated burst of bubbles. The line has caught in the air hoses that rise up over his right shoulder. The lines have become entangled, and the more he fights to free himself, the tighter they become, the more the sound of es-caping air increases.

His regulator grows stingy with its release of breathing air.

And now John Ackerman is just about as close to complete panic as he has ever been. But he remembers Henderson's ad-monition. Time and again: NEVER PANIC. It comes to him now, out of habit: Henderson's voice drilling the mantra into him, reinforcing the *Cave Diving Manual*'s reference to "the cas-cade of events. If you are in a spot where there is no margin for error, you will execute a flawless dive if you slow down and re-main in charge of your head."

Never panic. The minute you panic is the minute you give your life over to something else entirely. Fate. God. Unholy chance. The Dragon. Something other than the best tools you have to free yourself: your own hands guided by your own rea-son. Because down here there is no room for error. One wrong move can leave you pondering the last minutes of your life breath by breath.

He tries to choke back fear. He tries to breathe. The more he tries to break the cord, the tighter it becomes, the more air escapes out of his tangled hose, and the less of it he has flowing through his regulator, the harder it is to breathe. Ackerman eases, just a little, trying to think. And the sound of escaping air diminishes. His unobstructed airflow returns. He eases more completely, and the sound of escaping air stops.

At least he has a minute to think, to take stock. He is in blackout conditions, hopelessly entangled in several yards of nylon cord. He is breathing harder. Fear caused his heart rate to skyrocket and his near panic flooded his blood with adrenaline and the increased surge of energy made him breathe harder and use much more air than he normally would. He tries to think. He is deep underground in a cavern he glimpsed for the first time five minutes ago. And now he is totally blind. He is trussed up like a bug in a web, each subsequent knot on a different part of his body, his equipment. To make a single move in any direction only tightens his nylon net. He tries not to think about his air running out, about death coming out of darkness to perch at the edge of this black passage and wait for its prey to tire.

Ackerman summons all his reserves, and now he tells himself he has to think. He has to calm himself and think. Because he has no intention of making this underground world his watery grave. Just two days ago he celebrated his forty-seventh birthday with his wife and three children. And he is going to return to the surface to see them. He is damn well going to celebrate more birthdays. He has to pause and think.

And then he remembers what the passage was like when he

entered it. Every step of his eighty-foot swim was clear, at least when he entered. He does not know if he has enough air left to wait for it, but he tells himself if he can just stay calm long enough, if he can make himself still, he will not only use less oxygen, but the slow current of water out of this passage should eventually clear out the silt, and he will be able to see again. And once he can see, he can switch on his underwater light and figure out how to free himself. If he can see, he tells himself, he will get clear of this cord and return down the passage, cross the diving bell room, and swim up the chute to safety.

So against every thought in his head, every urge in his gut screaming at him to move and pull and twist and fight his way clear, Ackerman calms himself, forces his mind quiet, tells himself he has a plan. He will wait for the water to clear itself. And then he will disentangle and rise to the surface to safety.

He inhales, and the air fills his lungs.

He exhales, and the bubbles rise somewhere into the blank oblivion above him.

He waits . . .

2
Gunpowder
West Side bluffs, St. Paul
Sunday afternoon, March 21, 2004

Karl Schaak's foot strikes something solid and unexpected. The three explorers are nearly a hundred feet inside the massive cave complex, almost to the end of a cavernous eighty by-twenty-foot room. Their flashlights glimmer through the dark. Everything in this room filled with old industrial detritus gives off a different shade of gray or black. A large wooden crate, blackened by fire, is turned on its side. Small metal canisters are stacked haphazardly along one wall and near the room's center. Other metal tubes are strewn over the sand floor. Hydraulic hoses and random wiring twist over the debris. The walls are mottled with reinforced columns and brick. But even in here, where old trash mixes with newer cigarette butts, bottles, wrappers, and beer and soda cans, finding something buried is a little odd, a little interesting, which is just one of the reasons Karl, Jessica Stafford, and Alex Nelson have come into these caves.

The solid edge at Karl's feet could be the start of anything. A can, an old wooden box, maybe a crate of Civil War carbines, he wonders. Or some other kind of treasure; wouldn't that be cool. Maybe a coffin lid? The idea makes him smile. He digs with his toe until he feels the firm edge move, just a little. Whatever it is feels wooden.

He takes off his backpack and rummages through their spare batteries, bottled water, chips, and candy bars. Karl is good with his hands. He likes tools. He rarely goes anywhere—particularly into a cave complex like this one—without at least a couple of basic implements. Now he pulls out a standard screwdriver and sets the pack to one side.

"Shine a light down here, would you?"

Alex and Jessica shine their lights onto the off-white sand.

Karl drives the screwdriver into the soft cave floor, working its tip along the solid edge. He digs around the piece, disturbing more mottled sand. An odor comes up with the sand, something he thinks he recognizes. But the slightly sweet, peppery, organic smell doesn't make sense, buried this deep in a cave.

The wood feels like the cornered edge of an old crate. And it's loose—just a piece. When he finally frees it, he can see letters stenciled onto its side. He stands up to get a better look.

"Gimme some more light," he says.

Alex flashes his beam along the crate edge.

Karl brushes away more dirt and sand and squints at the faded print. But the words are incongruous, buried in a downtown St. Paul river bluff. He's uncertain he's reading it correctly. He brushes away more sand and squints to be sure. And then he exhales.

"I'll be goddamned," he says, a little fear mixed in with his surprise.

Karl and Jessica share a lower apartment in a triplex across the Mississippi River. Just a couple of hours earlier, near dusk, sitting in their place at 212 McBoal, the three of them were trying to decide what to do with the rest of their Sunday afternoon. "We could check out those caves," Karl suggested.

The day was cool and overcast, with a brisk wind scudding across the Mississippi River. By late afternoon, a narrow band of sunlight peeked through the clouds, but it wasn't enough to push the mercury over 32 degrees.

After kicking around other ideas, the three realized it had been a while since any of them have explored the caves. Like many of St. Paul's youth, the three have known about the caves since they were kids. They've located some entrances to caves they consider large and safe enough to enter. You never knew what might turn up, walking through those passages and rooms. Like most caves, they contained enough dark unknown to be interesting, maybe even a little scary. And these were urban, man-made caves. They'd been around for as long as any of them could remember, sometimes providing storage, sometimes shelter, more recently party places for the city's youth. They were concealed behind woods on the river bottom and difficult to patrol.

The authorities were always warning people to stay out of the caves. But the three explorers know the authorities warn people to stay out of all kinds of places they don't know anything about, because of an overarching sense of *potential liability*. In just one of their efforts to seal the caves, St. Paul officials invited building contractors to use the massive underground complex of tunnels and rooms—with interconnecting passages—as a dumping ground for construction debris. And since some of the ventilation shafts, drilled into the bluff to keep clean air flowing through the airtight St. Peter sandstone, were wide enough for a kid to squeeze through, they plugged those, too.

Unfortunately, the city filled *just some* of the extensive, sometimes interconnected cave system. There were plenty of rooms and passages still open enough to explore. These open sections were intermixed with the debris-filled rooms. Homeless people and kids sometimes used the handy wooden debris to build fires. In these caves, where the temperature is a constant 47 degrees and where there is not even a trace of light, fires provide warmth, solace, and illumination. Dangerous amounts of carbon monoxide could build up in the sealed-off rooms or seep into the tunnels like a snake nosing through a twisting burrow.

But Karl, Alex, and Jessica know about carbon monoxide and what causes it. If they ever see smoke or smell the remnant of an old fire, they don't enter the place. And on this day they're going into one of the largest cave complexes, with big openings in the sides of the cliff. The brewery caves, four stories high, could be a little dangerous, but that's what made them interesting.

Karl, Jessica, and Alex take their usual precautions. Karl puts together a small pack, and they all make sure they have bright, operational flashlights with backup batteries, just in case.

It's a five-minute drive to the caves, just across the river where Ohio Street winds down through the bluff and ends at Plato Boulevard. Karl scouts out a place to park. The river bottom between the bluff and the Mississippi is broad and high enough above the waterline to house several warehouses and businesses with large, old parking lots empty on a Sunday night. They choose one and drive across the cracked blacktop, parking near the bluff.

From Wabasha Street, where the West Side bluff begins, all the way down to the Smith Avenue Bridge and the start of Cherokee Regional Park—a distance of more than a half mile—the cliff face is honeycombed with man-made caves. Behind the Department of Agriculture building they have passed a warning sign so often they now ignore it, the white letters on the three-by-three-foot red metal background part of the colorful landscape. The warning talks about kids who died in one of the caves, a long time ago, from carbon monoxide poisoning.

Before dusk, Karl, Jessica, and Alex lock their car and walk back down Plato Boulevard, turn up Ohio Street, and start climbing the blacktop road, keeping a wary eye out for patrol cars. The brewery caves are directly across the river from the rise of St. Paul's offices, apartments, and warehouses and the old Ramsey County Jail. The neighborhood on top of the bluff stretches away from the city's center in several blocks of homes. But down here, where the street bends right, rising up the bluff, there is a narrow ravine cut into the left side of the cliff face. A wide path—probably an old brewery road—bisects the small patch of woods.

The three rise to the small path. They take one last look around, wait for a car to pass, and then duck down the wooded path. Back in under the trees, a couple of entrances to the old Yoerg Brewery caves are tucked into the cliff base.

On this late afternoon, sun breaks through the leafless branches. Blotches of light shine along the bluff face. A few spots of sunlight illuminate the sand floor just inside the cave opening. Otherwise the gaping, irregular maw at the base of the West Side bluff is completely black.

Some of the neighborhood kids call this the Al Capone Cave, but Karl knows that's "just a bunch of malarkey." Alex, who grew up in St. Paul, doesn't care what they call it.

This particular cave complex is *not* the kind of place most would enter. The soft sandstone bluff face and cave entrance are covered with graffiti. A large blue F looms over the cave entrance, maybe the start of the familiar expletive. There is a black B to one side, the rest of the letters marred by recent scraping. And there is a blue M and a G, though the word is obscured by a ten-foot spread of meltwater or last summer's rain, coming down from the top of the bluff. When the water drained off the cliff it mixed with dark earth and separated into several rivulets, leaving behind a black stain. Now its tentacles stretch over the yellowed sandstone, reaching into the sand at the base of the bluff.

Jessica snaps a picture and pockets her camera.

"Let's check it out," Karl says, starting down over a hump of earth into the deep-set entrance.

At around six feet, two hundred pounds, Karl, twenty-four, is built thick and solid with intense hazel eyes. Alex, twenty, is a little shorter and slighter, but strong enough. Jessica, nineteen, is Karl's roommate and girlfriend. Jessica doesn't worry about entering the cave as long as she's with the two men.

Near the cave entrance, Alex is startled to see a purse toppled over on the ground, its contents strewn over the sandy soil.

"What the hell?" he wonders.

"Probably some young kid got scared," Karl suggests.

"Could have been stolen?"

The purse, splayed open like an overturned turtle with its insides hanging out, reminds Alex of the wariness he feels about entering the caves. Vagrants moving along the Mississippi River sometimes use these caves for shelter, to get in out of the rain or cold.

The three step over the threshold and flick on their flashlights. Almost instantly a group of kids appears out of the darkness, laughing and hustling to get outside.

"Goddamn," Alex says, startled.

The kids barely look up, squinting and nodding as they exit into the late dusk light.

Not far into the cave there is a sharp turn to the left. Alex shines his light at a staircase dug into a soft sandstone passage and rising into darkness. Graffiti marks the walls. Kids have scratched all sorts of images into the soft stone, some obscure, some lewd and obvious. The place smells dank and earthen, but it is a noticeable 15 degrees warmer inside the caves.

Karl starts up the stairs. Alex marks the wall with a fresh X

Karl Schaak moves toward stairs inside a West Side cave. Courtesy Karl Schaak

they'll recognize and follows Karl up the steps. Jessica snaps another picture, and the three move farther into the dark.

"Check it out," says Karl, flashing his light into another opening.

The floor is covered by fine, off-white sand. The St. Peter sandstone is comprised of some of the finest quartz sandstone in the world. One of the first reasons people started digging here was to mine the sand, almost 100 percent pure silica, for making glass and cement.

Almost five hundred million years ago, the Ordovician sea broke over what is now the central United States. That ancient sea deposited a hundred-foot layer of white quartz sandstone. The rock is unusual because of its uniform grain size and single mineral composition. While the quartz sand grains are very hard, they are poorly cemented together, making it soft enough to mine easily. And the resulting deep holes in the cliff face were sometimes used for shelter, storage, growing mushrooms, even brewing beer.

In 1871 German immigrant Alexander Yoerg moved his fledgling brewery, one of the first in Minnesota, to this bluff face. The area had everything he needed to produce what would become the region's most sought-after beverage. There was plenty of water, and a good growing season yielded ample hops and barley. But to produce lager, which had a finer head of foam than the area's first beers, the brewing had to occur in a refrigerated space. The constant 47-degree cave temperature was ideal.

Over the next hundred years, the Yoerg Brewery dug extensive tunnels, shafts, and rooms into the soft St. Peter sandstone. The abandoned four-story underground maze—with storage rooms and production spaces—has the feel of a large

The Yoerg Brewery off Ohio Street, about 1910. Courtesy Minnesota Historical Society

dark labyrinth. The complex contains cavernous rooms, a ladder climbing up a cylindrical shaft to a second level, another level accessed by a hanging rope, handholds and footholds dug into the soft sandstone, large round ventilation shafts, and the industrial detritus from nearly a century of brewing fine German lager.

In 1952, when the brewery closed, the front facades and building tucked up against the bluffs were taken over by the Harris Plumbing Company until September 26, 1958, when the entire structure was razed after a massive conflagration. But the labyrinth of underground passages had never been entirely filled in or sealed up.

After ascending the stairs, examining some ventilation shafts, peering into an overhead tunnel with a rope hanging down, and finding a room stuffed with all kinds of debris—so much it cannot easily be entered—the three finally make their way to the rear of the large room, stepping over hydraulic hoses, twisted wires, and metal canisters and around the massive, burned wooden crate. Near the right side, halfway back, Karl discovers something buried in the dirty sand. When he digs it out, brushing off the crate edge, about the only thing he can say is, "I'll be goddamned."

"What?" Jessica says. "What's it say?"

"'Smokeless powder for a 4.2-inch mortar,'" he reads. There is a serial number, a lot number, its gross weight (fifty pounds), and its date of manufacture: 1952.

"Incredible," he adds. He hands the crate edge to Jessica and then bends down and starts digging around the place where the wood came up. "Shine that light," he says.

Jessica and Alex return their beams to the cave floor. Karl

digs down a few more inches, and there is a clear delineation where the color of sand turns from an off-white to almost black. When he brushes away more sand, he raises old burlap. If he pulls at the sack, it disintegrates. When he brushes a little deeper, more of the pungent smell drifts into the dank room.

Karl lived in South Carolina until he was thirteen. Down south he had many opportunities to handle fireworks. He and his buddies also did a little target shooting, and sometimes the aroma from the fireworks or ammunition would drift up into the warm southern air. He's pretty sure what's coming up in this cave is the smell of gunpowder. That means a powerful explosive is buried in this urban cavern. Overhead, he thinks he remembers a day care center and residential streets with houses stretching back into one of St. Paul's oldest neighborhoods.

"This can't be," he says.

Karl remembers the way very small amounts of gunpowder burn: hot and fast, with an intense flare that fires rockets into the night sky or propels lead slugs into a target. If a flame touches this powder, there could be quite an explosion under the bluff. Or one hell of a blow.

"You think it's been here since '52?" Jessica asks.

"That's when it was made," Karl says. "Probably sometime not long after, judging by the condition of these sacks."

"These caves have been abandoned as far back as I can remember," Alex comments.

"I wonder why they buried gunpowder in a cave?" Karl asks.

"Probably won't fire," Alex guesses. If it's been here that long and never been touched off, with vagrants starting fires and kids partying and smoking in the place, it's reasonable to assume it might be inactive.

"But it's been buried," Karl says.

Karl has a passing interest in Civil War memorabilia. He remembers the story of a collector finding an old cannonball with its gunpowder still intact. The intervening years ground the coarse powder into fine black dust. When it was accidentally ignited, the explosion was ten times more powerful than it would have been had it blown in the nineteenth century. He tells his friends about it.

"Boom," he says, with affect. "One less Civil War collector."

The three of them spend over an hour carefully digging, brushing away the top layer of old sand. What they find amazes them. They're pretty certain there are at least six fifty-pound bags of old gunpowder buried under a few inches of cave sand.

Alex is surprised, but somehow it figures. He's often thought milling around in this maze of man-made caves is like walking through an old fire pit. "You never know what you're going to find," he observes. "There's all kinds of stuff in here. Old rocks. Bottles. Cans. Anything can turn up."

"They're definitely interesting," Karl agrees.

After they find the edge of the crate and partially unearth several bags of gunpowder, they pause to consider. It's around 8:00 on a Sunday night.

A group of teenagers enters the large room. Like Alex, Jessica, and Karl, they're in search of a little adventure—or just a place to smoke, drink, and hide. But they're a little less thoughtful than the three standing over the bags of gunpowder. One of them walks nearby and strikes a match, holding it to her cigarette, inhaling in the entombed darkness.

"Hey," Karl yells. "There's gunpowder here."

Startled, the three strangers move away. There are other places to explore in these caves, many more passages, tunnels, and rooms.

Finally they've had enough of their crude digging. It's time to take a break, return to the apartment, and retrieve Karl's entrenching tool, a compact military shovel that will make it easier to excavate the four-by-ten-foot rectangle. For Alex, it's time to head home. They move through the passages, following their wall marks until they come to the yawning entrance in the cliff. Across the river, St. Paul's lighted skyline rises into the black sky. A chill has entered the dark air, and they pause to have a quick smoke before returning to their car.

By 2:30 Monday morning, Karl and Jessica have unearthed ten fifty-pound bags of gunpowder. Although the burlap, nearly half a century old, is fragile as gossamer, each sack appears to be full of the old, black powder. The treasure hunters are tired. And Jessica is getting a headache, probably the result of the plugged ventilation shafts and limited air circulation. It's time to go home.

"We'll call the St. Paul police in the morning," says Karl on the way back to their car.

It's cold near the bluff. There is an eerie calm where the big river flows about a quarter mile away. On the return to their car, walking along Plato Boulevard, the night is deep and still, as though the world sleeps.

"The cops have a bomb squad," Karl says, thinking aloud. "They'll know how to take care of it." Meanwhile, he hopes no stupid kids smoking cigarettes or bums wandering along the river walk into the rear confines of that room and strike a match.

3
Escape
Odessa Spring, near Granger, Minnesota
Sunday, April 29, 2001

In the middle of the silted-out room, John Ackerman has time to consider his predicament. He tries not to move. He has pulled out enough nylon cord to have a free-floating web interfering with his movements and air intake. He has no visual cues so he cannot be certain his neutral buoyancy is actually keeping him stationary in the six-foot-by-four-foot, rough-hewn underwater chamber.

Chamber, he thinks. That's what this is. A little chamber of horrors.

Stop it. Stay quiet. Don't move.

Panic is the enemy of survival. If he does not want to stay down here for the rest of his short life, he will not let the rampant fire come out of the dragon's mouth. He will not yield to panic, to the terror.

So Ackerman forces himself to stay calm. He forces the beast back into its lair.

The only other sound is the steady exhale of his bubbles rising into dark oblivion, whichever way is up. And the inhale as he recovers his breath, waiting. The sound and feel of life-giving oxygen calms him in the underwater room. He blinks, trying to see in front of him. But the silt-out conditions haven't improved. Not yet.

He waits.

He has no way to know how much time passes. Two minutes, or ten? Somewhere in between. Maybe seven. Seven is a lucky number. But it feels like an unlucky eternity.

He forces himself to stay calm, centered, focused. He tries not to move.

In the safety of Henderson's apartment pool, they had turned out the lights and practiced line entanglement. But the pool was heated, there was no current, and the walls were smooth and white and almost within reach. If he became too entangled, he could simply surface, rise through the few feet of water above him into an open, dark room filled with air. A place where he could kick to one side and support his tangled bulk by holding onto the pool's edge. A place where he could take off his mask, remove his tank, regulator, and fins, and climb out of the water to breathe. And Mark was there. If he had trouble with his equipment, Mark could help him.

But now Ackerman is trapped. There *is* a way out—one he cannot see, touch, or feel—either behind him or in front of him. He believes the edge of nylon cord tangled around his left foot and left hand leads in the right direction. If he can wait until the water clears, he can follow that line to safety.

In these conditions, with the water visually impenetrable, Henderson would have trouble finding the dive reel line, anchored near the bottom of the chute. And it would be very difficult to first feel for the line and then follow it around the small obstruction into the vestibule room and then through that room into the twisting honeycombed passages Ackerman has taken to get here.

If he is going to survive, he is going to do it on his own.

So he keeps waiting.

Henderson's brief line entanglement lesson taught Ackerman one very simple rule. Don't get caught up in your line. Getting twisted up in feet, yards of nylon cord is a very, very dangerous development, something that can trigger doom.

Was there anything else to that lesson? He remembers Henderson twisting the nylon cord around his tank, hoses, appendages—all to demonstrate what diminished airflow and movement can do to you—at least in the bottom of a swimming pool. And he remembers the other lesson. Henderson told him that if he is unfortunate enough to become entangled, the only way he can ever hope to survive is to stay calm and *not panic.*

Okay, Ackerman thinks. I'm keeping still. I'm waiting for this chamber of horrors to clear.

But *chamber of horrors* is not the way to think about it. His blood thumping through his head. Not chamber of horrors, he thinks. It's a damn small cavity deep underwater beneath forty feet of solid rock, a coffin-lid, if he wanted to think of it in a way that might kindle panic.

The only way to address line entanglement is with calm, clear reasoning and deliberate action. And in this case that means to stop. Hover. Wait.

He is happy about the size of his tank. He hasn't been underwater for more than fifteen, maybe twenty minutes. At least he doesn't think so. There is a lot of air in an eighty-cubic-foot tank. Some of it, but not that much, was forced out when he was struggling with the line. He thinks he has a while. He can afford to wait a while longer.

But everything inside him screams against the idea of floating calmly in this black chamber.

Not chamber.

In this blacked-out, underwater room.

But the water isn't clearing!

He reminds himself he's been here many times. He has wedged himself into spaces so tight he became hopelessly stuck, unable to free himself. But in each of those instances, like Houdini, he devised an escape. Once he expended so much breath he reduced the size of his lungs, rib cage, chest, just enough to squeeze out to safety.

But he has never been underwater, breathing through an assisted tank with a regulator, trussed up like a bug in a spider's web.

Easy, he thinks. Stay calm. Float.

Ackerman waits for another small eternity before he realizes that the water is not clearing. Not at all. He has been so focused on the effort to remain perfectly calm it takes him a while to notice. But after several minutes this hole is still opaque, impenetrable, dark as steeped tea, because he is either making more movement than he thinks or maybe his bubbles are stirring silt off the ceiling and walls.

But he hasn't been moving. Maybe he is so far down inside this honeycombed passage the movement of water is practically stagnant. There are lots of side channels and small seepages where water can lose itself, diminishing its current to a crawl. He assumes that his world has remained turbid and blinding because there is simply not enough movement to flush it clean. A flush he could feel. Current he could feel. Even though he is covered in a dive suit and his hands are encased in seven-mil gloves, he knows he can feel water movement, when there is current.

What now?

He decides to abandon his wait-for-the-water-to-clear strategy. He simply cannot stay down long enough. And he is uncertain he can remain perfectly still in these conditions without knowing exactly how much air is left, how much time.

Maybe if I take off these fins, he wonders. Maybe some line will loosen up and be discarded with them.

So he reaches down and peels off first his right fin, then his left, entangled in the line. He can feel them drop. But there is so much line woven around his tank valves and lanyard, underwater flashlight and harness, the absence of fins makes no difference whatsoever. He is still trussed up in this accursed nylon web.

He pauses. Tank harness, he thinks. He remembers Henderson's line-cutting knife, the one he absently borrowed right before dropping down into this hole. The crooked blade is tucked into a snug sheath and attached to his harness with a two-inch strap. He can get that damn knife and start cutting. But he remembers how small it is and knows it could easily be dropped. These gloves give him warmth but rob him of his dexterity and sense of touch. Like picking up a dime wearing a pair of mittens. But without them, his exposed skin would grow numb and in less than a minute his fingers would slow and seize, unable to feel anything, especially a tool with a one-inch blade.

But it could work. He could cut his way out of this web and crawl back to safety. This chance comes at the edge of a razor-sharp stainless-steel blade, and he cannot afford to bungle it.

Don't drop it, he thinks. Even before he has been able to locate the small sheath and strap, he reminds himself: DO NOT DROP THE BLADE!

He works his way by muffled feel along the tank and then down the length of harness and finds the two-inch strap. He feels the sheath with its life-saving blade, and after careful, awkward fingering, he is able to get it out and open it.

He grips the small handle with his right hand, ready to start cutting.

Think!

Unless he is very, very careful, he could cut the line that

tethers him to safety. He cannot cut the taut end of the dive reel line, the end that stretches from his foot out toward the chute. It is his single connection to a safe exit and his survival.

So he reaches to where he assumes the end of the line runs back along the passage. He feels for the line with his partially tethered left hand and finds it. He grips it with his glove, but he is not really able to feel it. He can tug and feel the line go taut in front of him.

Now he can turn and with his body movement pull the entire tangled mess of line behind him so it also tightens. He can feel the mess attached to the dive reel grow taut. Now he can start cutting. He reaches out behind him with the small knife, barely able to feel anything in his gloved hand. But there's something. With its crook, this little knife is much better than a Marine's K-bar knife or some other big underwater blade. A larger blade could easily cut the nylon cord, but it could also easily cut his air hoses. With the small, crooked blade he will not catch or cut anything but the cord. And he cuts. He finds strands of the web all around him, around his lanyard and flashlight, and back behind him, trussing up his hoses and tank. Ackerman searches for the taut lines connecting the entanglement to the dive reel. And he cuts. He finds a line, swings his hand until the crook of the blade goes taut, and then puts more pressure on the blade, and he feels it snap. Then he moves to the next piece of line. By degrees he begins to sever himself from the underwater web. Ackerman doesn't yet dare contemplate freedom, escape, survival. For now he focuses, concentrates, thinks his way through the line-cutting process. Don't think about the future. Don't think about the surface, sunlight, escape, freedom, survival, open air, the warm late April afternoon. Cut. Cut carefully.

Finally, his trussed-up body loosens. He no longer feels tethered to the dive reel that fell into the abyss and became lodged somewhere behind him. He believes he has freed himself, at least enough so he can swim and crawl away from this underwater skein. Now he pulls with his left hand, the one holding the connecting line to the escape chute.

But he feels nothing! He tugs, but there is no pressure, no tightness. What happened to the line leading back to the exit chute? Where's the goddamn line he was gripping just two minutes earlier, before he started cutting? He cannot feel it! He cannot believe he cannot feel it.

He knows better than to open his palm. He knows he cannot panic. Think! If the small cord is still being gripped but he cannot feel it because of his insulated diving gloves . . . then if he opens his hand to search for it, the line might as well have dropped into oblivion. He'll never be able to recover it, never be able to follow it out. He cannot open his hand and search for the wayward cord. He pulls and pulls again, arching back—at least what he thinks is backward—as much as this space allows, trying to back up in the small space, actually backing up closer to where he remembers setting the dive reel on the underwater ledge.

And then he is rewarded by the blessed return of pressure, the tug. The escape line goes taut. In his cutting fury, he must have floated down the length of passage toward his exit and slackened the nylon cord.

He takes a second now to re-stow his knife.

Recovered from the momentary fright, he begins following the line, pulling it with his hands, careful to keep it in his grasp, following it cautiously toward his exit. He moves slowly, deliberately, maintaining enough tautness in this line to keep it straight and true. His one true exit. He doesn't know how well Henderson anchored the other end of the line in the copse of rock near the bottom of the escape chute. If he didn't secure it well, the line could pull free. Or worse, if pulled too hard, it could scrape over some jagged underwater rock edge and break.

So he is very careful. He moves another foot through the underwater passage.

And then he feels a tug on his right foot! He is certain of it. At first it scares the hell out of him. In the next instant he knows it must be Henderson. Somehow Mark has found his way into this passage and come in to rescue him. But how did Henderson get below and behind him?

And then suddenly his head strikes the cave ceiling with blunt force. It hurts him, shocks him. Stunned, he tries to understand it. What's happening? And then he begins to realize.

His weight belt has a quick-release handle. The web's tangles must have popped it open, allowing the belt to fall off and wrap itself around his foot before dropping to the chamber floor. It felt like Henderson's warm tug, and Ackerman was going to lead them both to safety—and then he hit his goddamn head!

What more? What more could go wrong?

Ackerman breathes. He still holds the line firmly, carefully. Hauling his tank and harness behind him, he moves deliberately through the underwater passageway delicate pull by delicate, taut pull. If it pulls free, he'll be left down here to find a way out by feel and luck. And luck is a bad thing to depend on. Leaning on luck in conditions like these is like hoping you'll win the lottery to pay your rent.

But the line holds. He follows it hand over hand until he's

pretty certain he is passing through the underwater vestibule. He thinks it's beginning to clear, but even this chamber is still too silted-in to see more than a foot or two in front of his face.

Finally he thinks he must be near the chute when the line disappears into the cave floor. He feels around the line, around the rock where the line stops, but all he finds is solid rock. Impossible!

Think!

Don't drop the line.

Think!

Was this where Mark anchored the line? Did he tie it into the side of some rocks? Ackerman gropes around the end of the line, his legs in the air, his tank floating beside him in its makeshift harness. The exit chute must be near. He feels around the rock for where the line doubles back on itself. He tries to feel for some kind of opening, but there is nothing. Only the same silted water, maybe a little lighter, maybe a little clearer. His tank drifts to his side, and he searches among the rocks.

Finally John Ackerman looks up, and in an afternoon of cave diving filled with terrible surprises, one after the other, lining up like nightmares through a bad sleep, he sees a light shining through the turbid water. Shining down right above him, on top of him. The light grows more intense, and it can only mean one thing. Henderson has finally started to worry. Mark is descending the escape chute to look for him, and his light is showing the way.

And then Ackerman finds the small hole leading into the bottom of the chute. He enters it, pulling himself through it. He breathes steadily in the tight quarters, ascending. He follows Henderson's flashlight up the chute.

And finally John Ackerman emerges into the clear light of the warm April afternoon. He takes off his regulator and doffs his mask and squints into the afternoon light. And he breathes. He breathes in the spring air, and he thinks it is the sweetest air he has ever tasted.

The first thing Ackerman did after surfacing was describe his near-death experience. But—true to his single-minded pursuit—he highlighted what he considered to be the necessary changes they had to make in their exploration. For starters, he instructed Henderson to return into the chute with a heavy nylon rope attached to a crowbar. Something they'd be able to easily find, pick up and feel, regardless of water clarity or conditions. Something that wouldn't become entangled.

Once the heavy nylon rope was in place, they stopped long enough to let the water clear.

Ackerman, still fixated on trying to locate the doorway, put off thinking about his near brush with death. When the water finally cleared, he re-entered the spring, moved along the heavy cord, and even returned to his small chamber of horrors. He peered over the edge of the diving reel rock ledge and saw the pile of white line floating eerily behind the wedged reel. It was unnerving.

He also resolved to bring another experienced diver back with him the next time they came down to explore the underwater passage.

On May 10, 2001, Phil Gemuenden, an experienced wreck diver from Duluth, joined Henderson and Ackerman on another underwater exploration of the spring.

After April 29, Ackerman had come to appreciate more fully the near miss of his earlier dive. Had he not asked to take the dive knife and remembered it at the moment he had no other alternatives, he would probably have died. After two weeks of reflection, he decided to leave the initial cave exploration to the experts.

Henderson and Gemuenden went into the chute, following the thick nylon cord into the water-filled passage. Because Gemuenden was inexperienced in cave diving, Henderson wanted him to understand silt-out conditions. Halfway into the passage it was almost entirely dark, and he signaled Gemuenden it was time to return to the surface. But when Henderson exited the chute, Gemuenden was nowhere to be found.

Ackerman and Henderson waited on the surface for fifteen minutes before the determined Lake Superior diver returned.

Gemuenden had continued along the passage, exploring past and through Ackerman's chamber of horrors. The water had not yet silted out. Another ten feet beyond the dive reel shelf, the passage rose slightly and then closed off completely in a boulder choke. It was a dead end.

Ackerman was disappointed but not surprised by the news. On April 29, before the chamber silted in, he thought he saw the passage ahead rise up, but he couldn't be sure. He *believed* Gemuenden, but of course he had to see for himself.

After a while, the passage cleared enough so he could re-enter the spring. Using the thick nylon cord, he retraced his dive to the chamber and went far enough beyond to verify Gemuenden's conclusion. This time Gemuenden was with him, and when Ackerman returned to the surface, Gemuenden stayed down and continued exploring. In another fifteen minutes he returned to report he'd found a wide gap in the floor where water was pushing up with a strong current.

They waited until the water began to clear, and then Gemuenden re-entered the spring.

John Ackerman's dive journal entry conveys Gemuenden's final, grim assessment.

The long surface wait seemed to drag on forever. I was having flashbacks about my previous near death experiences and was very nervous that Phil may be in a desperate situation. Finally, I felt a tug on the rope and saw the telltale bubbles which indicated that Phil had made it safely to the exit chute. Phil described how he had worked his way through the constriction, went ahead, then dropped down through another restriction and went straight down, only to fail at this attempt to slip through a continuation of the floor crevice that had been spanning part of the cave floor. He said he was extremely lucky to have made it out alive. For reasons unknown, he did not drag the safety line with him; so attempting to find his way out, in total blindness through a series of complicated squeezes, was part luck and part desperation to survive. (He was livid that Mark did not join him part way into the cave and at least hold the light above the first constriction.)

Soon after, Phil returned to the cave to retrieve Mark's reel, which had never been taken out. I also returned to the main passage (two times) to obtain several compass readings and then bid this mysterious underground abyss farewell. Sometime before the end of the summer, when the water is almost stagnant, we hope to return with a large water pump. It is hoped we can lower the water level enough to create an air space at the back end so the rock slope can be probed . . . hopefully revealing a dry upper level. A long shot, yes. But that's how this game is played.

At the spring near Granger along the Minnesota-Iowa border, John Ackerman was wrong about his doorway to the Odessa. Or at least, he is quick to assert, it wasn't accessible via the narrow, twisting passages of the spring. But there *is* a doorway down there . . . somewhere. And Ackerman believes he will find it.

4
The Authorities
West Side bluffs, St. Paul
Monday afternoon, March 22, 2004

Because Karl and Jessica were awake until just about dawn, it is midday before they rise and make their first call. Karl knows the authorities don't want anyone in those caves, but he has to make the report. That much gunpowder set deep into the West Side bluff could cause an explosion that might rival the

Oklahoma City bombing. They look up the general number for the St. Paul police, and Karl dials it. When he finally gets to an on-duty officer, he explains where they were and what they found. The officer's response is unexpected.

"We found gunpowder in those old caves," explains Karl. "We can show you. Around five hundred pounds."

"You found what, where?"

Karl repeats his story about the powder. About how they found it, where it is, and the inherent danger of having that much live powder (maybe even more) buried beneath a residential neighborhood.

"Yeah, right," the officer says, apparently thinking it's a crank call, and hangs up.

"They don't believe us," he tells Jessica.

He still has the crate edge he brought away from the caves. Their neighbor Charlie, who lives upstairs, has come down, and they've shown him their discovery, told him how they'd spent the wee hours of last night and this morning unearthing the stash of powder under the bluff.

Charlie suggests they call Fort Snelling, where the Army Reserve has a regional command. "This is military stuff. Maybe someone out there would know about it."

Jessica and Karl decide to call the media as well. If the St. Paul cops won't believe them, maybe one of the news channels will.

Charlie uses his cell phone to call the fort, while Jessica opens the phone book and starts looking up the numbers for the news channels.

After introducing himself and explaining about his need to speak with someone about gunpowder, Charlie is transferred to an appropriate contact. He relates the story of finding the gunpowder buried in the St. Paul caves, reading the crate edge to the man. "It says, 'Smokeless powder for a 4.2-inch mortar.'" He reads him the serial and lot numbers. "'Date of manufacture,'" he concludes, "'1952.'"

For a moment the other end of the line is quiet.

"Hello?" Charlie asks.

"Goddamn it!" the man blurts.

"What?"

There's another long pause while the voice at the other end collects itself. "I mean, I spilled my coffee here. Spilled some coffee on myself. Just a minute. Let me get a pencil and some paper, and you can give that to me again, a little slower? And I need your contact information."

Charlie repeats the words from the crate edge. He relates the story of where the gunpowder was found, buried in the sandy cave floor. He thinks the Fort Snelling official is a little stunned, and he wonders if the man really spilled coffee—or recognized the powder and knew what it was. He gives the man Karl and Jessica's contact information and hangs up.

"That was weird," he says, laughing. He describes the official's reaction to Karl.

Jessica is finishing up her last media call. She's managed to contact the three big local TV stations, WCCO, KARE, and KMSP, and they're all a little interested.

She starts sharing the media's comments when their phone rings.

Karl picks it up. "Hello?"

"This Karl Schaak?" It's an older voice across the line, military formal.

"Yes?"

"This is Sergeant Stone from Fort McCoy in Wisconsin. I'm in EOD. Do you know what that is?"

It takes him a moment to remember. "Explosives Ordnance Disposal?" Karl says.

"That's right. I understand you have some smokeless powder on your hands? For a 4.2-inch mortar?"

Karl tells the story of how and where they found the crate edge. He reads the crate's lettering to the sergeant and gives him the serial and lot numbers and the year of manufacture. He tells the sergeant they've phoned the St. Paul police, but the police don't believe him.

When Karl is done, Sergeant Stone takes a millisecond to respond. "Karl," he starts, "you call the St. Paul police back. Now don't be shy about using your most authoritative voice. You tell them Sergeant Stone from EOD at Fort McCoy told them they better get their goddamn butts down to have a look at that stuff. And I mean now. And you tell them as soon as they get down there they should give me a call. Take down this number," he orders.

Karl writes it all down. Finally, they're getting somewhere.

Karl does as the sergeant asked. Using the EOD expert's advice, he convinces a patrol officer to meet them near the bluff.

A half hour later, Karl and Jessica are waiting in the afternoon light for the St. Paul police officer. They're at the intersection of Plato Boulevard and Ohio Street, near the entrance to the caves, when they see a patrolman's cruiser making a slow turn along the blacktop. They're expecting the cruiser to pull in and park near the caves, but it slowly rounds the corner and just keeps going.

"Hey!" Karl says. "He's not even stopping."

The cruiser makes a return pass, and this time Karl and Jessica step out into the street and wave him down.

The officer pulls up but doesn't park his patrol car or get out.

"You the officer checking on the gunpowder?"

"Yup. But I don't see it," he says.

Karl and Jessica figure that either the St. Paul police don't believe them—think it's a hoax—or this officer doesn't have any familiarity with the caves. No wonder kids like to use them for parties. Maybe the police just leave them alone.

Fortunately, Karl has brought the crate edge with him, and he shows it to the officer. "You have to get out of your car and walk into the cave. It's in the cave," Karl explains.

The officer looks annoyed, but the proof of the old piece of wood with lettering finally convinces him to pull the cruiser into a lot and park. The officer follows them to the cave entrance, his full gear rattling on his belt and his radio box stuck to his front shoulder. He looks awkward, walking up Ohio and turning onto the old brewery path through the trees. And when he sees the entrances, he's understandably reluctant to enter the caves. But there is no other way. He reminds them the caves are off-limits. It is illegal to enter them, and they shouldn't have been in there. After they nod and assure him they won't enter them again, they guide him to the disintegrating bags of gunpowder. The officer takes one look at the open pit and expels a deep breath.

"We've gotta get the bomb squad in here."

They spend only a few minutes in the cave, circling over the dug-out rectangle of cave floor long enough to size up the bags and powder. The officer doesn't like the smell or feel of the place, and he's beginning to understand just how potentially lethal the stash of powder might be. Judging from the cigarette butts and scorched wood lying around, coming in contact with a flame is not so much a matter of *if* but *when*.

He radios in the call and waits by the entrance, making sure no one enters.

Within an hour the place is swarming with St. Paul's bomb squad specialists. Before anyone goes in, they don their gear: full helmets, bulletproof vests, heavy black boots, and breathing devices. They have firsthand experience with these death traps. Some of the officers still remember the two girls who went into the caves late one night in 1992 and didn't come out, at least not alive. In another nearby cave, in 1989, they removed the remains of a man who had set up house, complete with cooking stove and utensils, in the earthen room. A fire in a mattress inside the cave created dangerous levels of carbon monoxide, and the vagrant was overcome.

The police are stunned by what they find. By the end of the day their thorough search has yielded another nearby stash of the old bags, this one filled with almost a thousand pounds of old gunpowder.

Over the next two to three days, there is a frenzy of media coverage on what Karl, Jessica, and Alex unearthed. The local channels cover it on the evening news, and articles appear in the *St. Paul Pioneer Press* and *Star Tribune*. One *Pioneer Press* article discusses how the caves have been used for everything from brewing beer and aging cheese to storing gunpowder. Tracey Baker, a librarian at the Minnesota Historical Society, noted, "There was all kinds of stuff stored over there. . . . They were, literally, a cool place to store things. There are still caves all over the country where people are storing microfilm. It's cheap."

St. Paul police spokesman Paul Schnell repeated what the police know from bitter experience: "We discourage people from going into the caves due to significant safety concerns and potential health concerns."

Karl, Jessica, and Alex consider themselves fortunate. They went into the caves on a Sunday night, looking for a little excitement and adventure, and they discovered both. And after only a little consideration, they knew they had to inform the authorities, who dragged their collective feet but eventually responded appropriately. But not completely.

For a few days in late March 2004, the media coverage of the cave discoveries blanketed Minnesota. While most hoped it would dissuade others from entering the caves, it was interesting to ponder what else might be found in this far-flung labyrinth of tunnels and old rooms. In homes and schoolrooms or riding in cars after class, all over the metro area, there were kids mulling the peculiar mix of attraction, danger, and adventure St. Paul's man-made caves might provide. They were interested in finding treasure, or at the very least an afternoon's thrill by climbing into the holes that reached deep beneath the city. And like legions of kids and vagrants, they barely acknowledged the three-by-three-foot glaring red aluminum sign, passing it during their search up the overgrown hillside for another entrance into the mysterious catacombs. It reads,

> Jill Huntington and Annie Fries never graduated, never turned 18. Both died from carbon monoxide poisoning in these caves on September 26, 1992. Carbon monoxide poisoning is a real possibility to trespassers in these caves.
> PLEASE STAY OUT!

PART TWO

A Perfect Storm

Fandell's Cave, West Side bluffs, St. Paul,
2004

The last class for the Cedar Alternative School ends at 2:10. Like most of the other students in the Burnsville-Eagan-Savage School District, these five are probably happy to see their final session of the day. Jay Boucher, Justin Jensen,

Patrick Dague, Nick Larson, and Natalie VanVorst trail out of school toward Natalie's tan Chevy Cavalier.

Sometime—perhaps on the morning drive to school, or over lunch, or in the hallway between classes, or in the parking lot just after school—the five teenagers decide they're going to explore one of the caves in St. Paul. Patrick Dague believes he knows about a new cave none of them have yet entered. And like many teenage decisions, the idea to explore this new cave has more spontaneity than thoughtfulness.

All of them have been to the caves before and know they contain something inexpressible, compelling, maybe even a little dangerous. The caves are *not* part of the suburban landscape in which these five reside. They are dark, mysterious, and filled with all kinds of junk—most of it from some other time. Their walls are marked with graffiti, and some of them are dank and stale and smell a little. But they're definitely interesting. And the idea that there's another cave in that St. Paul bluff they haven't explored gives a sense of adventure to an otherwise overcast, cool Tuesday afternoon.

Accounts of the number and size of the caves along St. Paul's bluffs differ, in part because there are so many. Most of them are former sand mines. There are eighty-one mine entrances between Wabasha Street and Lilydale. Approximately thirty of them, with thirty-seven entrances, are interconnected passages at the lower end of this stretch, between Wabasha and Ohio streets. Twenty-four of these are dead-end tunnels, some containing side tunnels connected to adjacent shafts; two contain complexes with rooms, pillars, and interconnecting tunnels; only one opens into a small space. Most contain backfill, which makes it difficult to measure their dimensions, but a 2005 engineering report estimates that "Most mines are between 13 feet and 19 feet wide, and between 12 feet and 30 feet high."

The teenagers want to enter a cave at the eastern, downstream end of this stretch.

Cedar is an alternative school. On the corner of Diffley and Nicols Road in Eagan, Minnesota, sits the one-story, nondescript brick structure where every year 160 to 190 tenth-, eleventh-, and twelfth-grade students attend the usual assortment of classes that for one reason or another did not work for them in the district's main high schools. It is a close-knit school.

Jay Boucher, nineteen, is the oldest of the five, ready to graduate this spring. He plays guitar and likes having friends over to the Boucher home in Savage. Patrick Dague, seventeen, has been at the school for two years and—like Nick Larson and Justin Jensen—is looking forward to a spring graduation. Patrick likes to joke, enjoys playing tricks on people, and, like many seniors, is having a hard time focusing on his last high school semester. On this day he has been absent from school, but he decides to join the others for a trip to the caves. Nick Larson is five feet ten inches and 150 pounds and just came to the school from Burnsville High in January. His eighteenth birthday is a little over a week away. He sometimes watches his younger brother and sister, and he likes to play video games and listen to rap music with friends. Like Nick, Natalie VanVorst has been at Cedar for only a semester. She's a junior. With long blonde hair and a penchant for stylish dress, she has acquired the nickname Ms. Hollywood. Her smile makes it fit. Justin Jensen is a skater and snowboarder and moved to Savage two years earlier, when he enrolled at Cedar. Before that he lived in different parts of the country.

Cedar's student body is drawn from all over the district. Four of the five kids trailing toward Natalie's 1997 tan four-door Chevrolet Cavalier are from Savage and have known each other from previous schools. Patrick came to the school from Burnsville, and in spite of his absence this day, he is still on track to graduate in June.

In most every way they are typical American teenagers pursuing typical adventures on a typical Tuesday afternoon. They are also unique human beings who walk and breathe and, if given the chance and time, will grow into adults who could very likely accomplish something significant. Sometimes the real mystery is that with all of life's dangers—hiking along cliff faces, swimming deep lakes, traversing thin ice, driving through fog or snow, and similar activities—so many of us survive our youth and grow up to marry, buy a house, raise a family, and grow old.

From the corner of Nicols Road and Diffley there are several ways to drive to St. Paul's bluffs. One of the simplest is to turn right on Nicols and drive a half mile to where the road bends right and becomes Cedarvale Boulevard. From there you can drive another half mile to Silver Bell Road. Turn left and then immediately right onto Highway 13 north, and for the next several miles the road runs along the Mississippi river bluff.

Presumably the five students crowd into Natalie's Cavalier and make their way along this bluff. A little more than nine miles from school, Highway 13 passes in front of a T intersection. Lilydale Road drops perpendicular to the right of the highway and descends down the bluff to the old river bottom woods, now Lilydale Regional Park.

There was a time neighborhoods crowded across this low-lying spread of land near the river. But it is part of a massive floodplain, and after the last big rise of water it was finally condemned and razed and turned into the park. This spring the maples, cottonwoods, and understory are already starting to leaf green.

The sky, which has been overcast most of the day, remains cloudy. After a very cold morning, the temperature has climbed almost 30 degrees, and it feels good to be out in the moderating warmth of spring after a day spent indoors. Riding in a car through the greening river bottom woods toward something a little different is a pleasant diversion from the worries of classrooms, teachers, parents, and whatever awaits them at each of their homes. The five teens are just going to have a little fun, a little adventure on a Tuesday afternoon.

Normally these caves are harmless. But this is one of those rare days when a series of factors and events—some ancient history, some well-meaning efforts by authorities, some as benign as late night news and barometric pressure—conspire to cause the worst kind of tragedy.

Man-made caves are not like wild caves. Natural caves like those in the world's limestone karst regions often have multiple entrances and small pockets that reach into other cavities or to the surface. Wild caves breathe. In fact, sometimes cavers will hold their hands in front of a small opening in the earth and feel a steady breath of wind. Not in every cave. The air in some can be stale and dangerous, sometimes containing pockets of bad gas. But most wild caves are naturally ventilated, to one degree or another.

Geologic forces have moved mountains since the Ordovician sea deposited its sandy remnant five hundred million years ago. On the surface of the bluff rests a layer of glacial till. Beneath the glacial till there is a fifty-foot layer of Galena limestone. Beneath the Galena layer rests another seventy-five feet made up of Decorah shale, Platteville limestone, and Glenwood shale. And beneath the Glenwood is the St. Peter sandstone.

With almost two hundred feet of layered rock above them, the caves dug out of the sandstone form sealed chambers. The early miners and those who used the leftover holes for growing mushrooms, aging cheese, brewing lagers, or cold storage knew these corridors and tunnels did not breathe. They almost always added ventilation shafts, some so large kids could use them as entrances to the now forbidden caves.

When the caves ceased being places of natural cold storage or food production, the St. Paul authorities knew they were potentially dangerous. Numerous efforts have been made to prevent people from entering the caves. "No trespassing" signs were posted. Open entrances were bulldozed or cemented over, some blockages reinforced with rebar. Ventilation shafts were filled. But the sandstone bluff can be dug out with a spoon and a little determination, and the entrances were never closed for long.

Filling the caves seemed a more permanent solution, but some of these spaces were extremely large, thirty feet wide with twenty-foot ceilings and longer than a football field. After a record flood on the Mississippi in April 1965, approximately two hundred houses on the river flats were condemned. Rather than haul the bulldozed debris to suburban landfills, much of it was used in attempts to fill the largest of the bluff caves. Rafters, siding, metal pipes, plaster, cement—everything was bulldozed into the largest cave entrances. The city had outstanding contracts with a few firms to pack the caves with noncombustible construction debris. The remains of Miller Hospital, one of St. Paul's largest, demolished in the mid-1970s, fills one cave. In more recent years, especially after the 1992 deaths of Jill Huntington and Annie Fries, there have been concerted efforts to fill the caves.

The authorities believed their efforts to plug the larger caves solved two problems. First, taxpayers would save money, both on hauling the debris to a landfill and on the space it would have taken. And second, the largest caverns would be filled up so they could not be entered.

Unfortunately, no one anticipated that after a short time the mounds of rubbish would settle, creating pockets of air space above, around, and throughout the massive piles. Also, wood and other combustible material that had been left in the caves or dumped with the fill provided plenty of convenient dry fuel for those who wanted a fire for solace or warmth.

E. Calvin Alexander, professor of geology and geophysics at the University of Minnesota, has noted that the presence of wooden debris means fires are inevitable. The burning process consumes oxygen and releases carbon monoxide. If material is burned in the sealed-off caves, the absence of ventilation creates a confined space where oxygen can be depleted and carbon monoxide can pool in higher than normal concentrations. Alexander has called these man-made caves "death traps."

And the caves have been in the news recently, in stories the young people driving toward these caves probably heard. Just a month earlier, Karl Schaak and his friends found almost a ton of military-grade gunpowder buried deep within the old Yoerg Brewery caves. On March 24, the *St. Paul Pioneer Press* carried an article entitled "Caves: Good for storing beer, cheese, gunpowder." Both major Twin Cities newspapers carried several such pieces, and local television and radio news channels also covered the cave discoveries.

Weather also plays a role. In some years, late April has seen little change in the trees or wild prairie grass growing along the Fort Snelling State Park river bottom and nearby golf course. But this year the season is early. The past week has been warm and overcast with a couple of days of intermittent light rain. The golf course is green, and the trees along the rise of hill through which Highway 13 passes are beginning to leaf out. Many of the houses in the neighborhoods along 13 have tulips rising out of their beds.

April 27, 2004, is remarkable for two reasons: temperature and barometric pressure. First, the start of the day is one of the coldest on record. Just before dawn, the thermometer settles at 30 degrees Fahrenheit. It hovers there for a cold, dark hour before starting to rise with the sun. And like many of these late April days, it spends the sunlight hours climbing. By the close of school, it is 57 degrees and still rising. After the freezing dawn, the rapid climb in temperature reminds everyone it is spring—particularly seventeen-year-olds who are themselves just starting to blossom. It is time to get outdoors and contemplate the permanent retirement of heavy coats.

Just after midnight, the barometric pressure is 30.11 in/1019 hPa. It holds there until around 10:00 AM and then begins a steady, precipitous decline. By 4:00 PM, it has dropped to around 29.85 in/1010 hPa and is still falling. When the barometric pressure outside a cave begins to rise, the air is pushed inside the cave. When the outside air pressure begins to drop, particularly when the fall in barometric pressure is dramatic, the air inside a cave is pulled out.

What little air passes in and out of the man-made caves along the bluff moves through narrow cave openings. The five teenagers will make their way to an underground passage with a small entrance, approximately three feet by two feet, that forms a kind of lip. At one time the entrance was covered over. Then the top of it was dug away so people could slip inside. It is like a small hobbit hole made at the top of a big door.

Since the air in the cave is being sucked out of the small cave entrance, whatever carbon monoxide exists in the lower parts of the cave—maybe even in small pockets near the surface inside the permeable sandstone walls—is being sucked into the cave's chambers.

The danger from carbon monoxide in St. Paul's caves is known to some. Dave Gerboth's graying hair, thick, tinted glasses, and deadpan conversational tone belie his more than eight hundred subterranean explorations, which he has recorded and cross-referenced in his own detailed cave journal database. At fifty-five, he is five feet ten and fit, with thick, muscled forearms and a strong back. He has not only explored most of the St. Paul caves, but he assisted the Minnesota Speleological Survey with early efforts to map them. He remembers entering a cave complex in the early 1980s behind what would become, by 2004, the Department of Agriculture building.

"At the time," Gerboth comments, "I was exploring the caves using a carbide lamp." Carbide lamps, still used by some cavers today, burn acetylene to produce an intense white light.

"In one of the mines where the entrance had been re-opened, there was a crawl space above all the construction debris the city deposited there. I remember the air was fairly clear. But my carbide lamp kept going out. I remember thinking the clear air was misleading, that there wasn't enough oxygen in the crawl space to keep my carbide lamp lit. If kids came into this tunnel with flashlights, they could pass out before they knew what happened."

Carbon monoxide gas is odorless, colorless, and poisonous. It is produced when a fire burns without enough oxygen to allow complete combustion. This can happen with oil, coal, wood, kerosene, natural gas, liquefied petroleum (LP) gas, and even charcoal. One of the most common sources of carbon monoxide is car exhaust.

Carbon monoxide takes the place of oxygen in the blood. In essence, people in environments saturated with carbon monoxide gas begin to suffocate, though they continue to breathe and do not realize they aren't getting enough oxygen to keep the brain and body working. If the air is particularly saturated with carbon monoxide, people can, without warning, be overcome and fall unconscious in a matter of minutes.

Symptoms include a mild headache, shortness of breath, nausea, dizziness, lethargy, and confusion. They can be slow coming on and easily mistaken for something as simple as the flu (without the fever) or a viral infection. And some people can first experience a mild euphoria, similar to the effect of one or two martinis.

In the weeks preceding April 27, fires were reported in some of the caves and the St. Paul Fire Department was called at least four times. On April 9, a team of firefighters investigated a fire in and around the caves between 5:24 and 6:40 AM.

James Syvertsen, the firefighter in charge, described the event: "Refuse fire in caves between Minnesota Department of Agriculture and St. Paul Cave nightclub. Smoke venting from small vent holes on side of hill. Conferred with chief #2 and decided to let it burn out. No admittance to caves for extinguishment. Later conferred with public works and parks department and decided to plug holes that are venting."

The fire was apparently large enough to send smoke out hillside vent holes. Rather than climb into a dangerous space and fight the fire with conventional efforts, the St. Paul Fire Department decided to close off any sources of oxygen to the caves and let the fire burn itself out. Observers claimed the fire burned for approximately a week before finally dying.

A little over twelve hours later, at 5:47 PM, another fire team, headed by Captain William "Bill" Lee, checked on the site. His comments state, "Smoke coming from cave was checked yesterday and today. . . . We were unable to enter, but used thermal imager to check for heat near the entrance. We noticed no hot areas near the entrance."

Presumably "yesterday" was actually the early morning hours of the same day. But again, there was no reason for the firefighters to enter the caves since, given time, the flames would consume the oxygen in the space. In effect, the fire would suffocate.

On Monday, April 12, at 6:58 AM, the firefighters were again called to the caves because of complaints about smoke in the area. In his remarks, Martin Ludden, the firefighter in charge, stated, "Smoke odor from a nearby cave fire. Building engineer will control problem with HVAC system." The address referenced in this incident is 90 West Plato Boulevard, or the Department of Agriculture building.

On April 19, 2004, firefighters again visited the caves. The firefighter in charge, Scott Case, stated, "Caves behind Group Health [HealthPartners] had smoke coming from two openings. We checked for extension and found none."

And finally, at 2:24 in the afternoon on Sunday, April 25, 2004, firefighter James Syvertsen again finds "Light smoke from small cave on hillside. Discussed with chief #2 earlier and decided on no entrance."

Whether this is the same fire as the one burning on April 9 or a different fire, one thing is clear: throughout much of April 2004, fires are burning in the series of caves behind the HealthPartners building and the Department of Agriculture building. And the fires are producing enough smoke to annoy or alarm workers in the nearby buildings.

The Occupational Safety and Health Administration (OSHA) standards for permissible amounts of carbon monoxide gas in working conditions "prohibit worker exposure to more than 50 parts of the gas per million parts of air averaged during an 8-hour time period." Other agencies, however, put the number for carbon monoxide exposure much lower. In 2004 the more conservative American Conference of Governmental and Industrial Hygienists (ACGIH) published guidelines of 25 parts per million (PPM) over an eight-hour period. The ACGIH went further, stating that the maximum exposure for thirty minutes should not exceed 75 PPM, or three times the threshold level value, and that no one should *ever* be exposed to more than six times the threshold level (150 PPM).

Sometime after 3:00 PM the afternoon of April 27, the five teens roll onto Plato Boulevard. The cave they are seeking is behind, a little to the right of, and approximately forty feet up the bluff from the Department of Agriculture building, a concrete and glass structure at 90 West Plato Boulevard. There is a large parking lot in front, but the glass atrium and solid bank of tinted windows along the four building floors make it easy to look out and watch someone park.

Next to the Department of Agriculture building, the HealthPartners clinic, 205 South Wabasha Street, has fewer windows and a larger parking lot. Some of the lot bends back behind the building, to the side of the main entrance, and is out of view. Natalie VanVorst finds a place to park there, and she and her friends get out of the car.

Carrying their flashlights, they step over a curb and cross a small patch of grass. A narrow path meanders along the slanted hillside below the bluff. The hillside was formed from fallen sand and rock and has long since been covered over by heavy growth, like much of the almost two-hundred-foot rise of bluff face. It is easy to follow the trail behind the buildings, winding along the bottom of the cliff.

Pat, Natalie, Jay, Nick, and Justin walk in back of the Department of Agriculture building. There are tinted windows in the rear of the building and a large section of poured concrete patio between the building and the start of bracken and tree growth. Near the bottom of the growth, as the hill starts rising, sits the three-foot-by-three-foot red warning sign about the carbon monoxide deaths of Annie Fries and Jill Huntington. But that happened twelve years earlier, when four of the five now peering up the hillside—searching for the opening to a cave they've never explored –were only five years old. It might as well have been a lifetime ago. And besides, these kids have seen and read the warning and still entered the caves. And every time they have emerged unscathed.

They peer up the hillside and one of them, perhaps Patrick Dague, who knows about this unexplored opening, points toward the black hole near the base of the cliff and starts to climb.

6
Misfortune
West Side bluffs, St. Paul
Tuesday, April 27, 2004, approximately 3:00 pm

What happened on and in that hillside over the next forty-five to eighty minutes is unclear. Published accounts and interviews provide some basic information, and other events can be conjectured.

Jay Boucher had been into the caves numerous times,

probably more than any of the others. While none of them had been inside this particular cave, since Jay was both an experienced spelunker and the oldest of the five, he may have been the first to enter. On the other hand, since Patrick Dague knew about the unexplored section and probably guided the group to the location, he may have led the way.

The cave entrance, a crude opening dug out of the soft sandstone face, allowed just one person through at a time. One account described it being as small as eighteen to twenty-four inches wide, another as large as three feet by three feet.

At one point the authorities tried to seal over the entrance with concrete, wire, and steel from an old bridge, probably the High Bridge, which was demolished in 1985 and whose debris several other accounts have said was shoved into many of the caves. If the entrance was covered over with steel and concrete, the smaller opening now dug into the cliff face was probably at the top of the original entrance.

Suburban kids coming to the heart of old St. Paul, one of the largest urban centers in the state, likely fear vagrants or a gang of urban youth more than getting trapped in the caves or being overcome by carbon monoxide. Whoever enters the cave first is probably on the lookout for any movement in the dark, any flicker in the shadows or rustle through the main cave entryway. But he sees only the waver of his own flashlight down the sloping pile of sand.

He may also see a slight haze, some thin wisps of smoke, remnants of one of the fires that had recently burned in the caves. In mid-April, another explorer who entered the caves in this vicinity had found the tunnels thick with smoke and a smell in the air like bad paint fumes. This explorer and his friends reportedly penetrated the caves for several feet before the conditions forced them to exit.

All five teens push through the narrow opening, one at a time. Once inside, they slide down the slope of sand. Just five feet inside the cave they are able to stand. They also feel the sharp drop in temperature, the comparative coolness of the dank, still air.

There must have been a bad smell in the air, at least something a little unpleasant. But it probably wasn't much worse than the mildew smells inside other bluff caves. A long light beam shining from the small cave entrance touches graffiti on the walls. Their flashlights play over the open space, shining into the darker, shadowy places, mostly ahead, disappearing into the darkness. Not far from the entrance sits a three-foot wall. They climb over the wall and keep exploring. A short way ahead, there is a wide room where the ceiling comes down to no more than four feet. They have to bend to walk into it. There is a huge pillar in its center, apparently holding up the low-hung ceiling.

Perhaps here one of them complains about the air, or feels light-headed, or has already been turned around enough to worry about being able to find the way out. So they all turn back, retracing their steps, climbing over the wall, scrabbling back up the sand slope toward the sunlight to the entrance, and pushing back out into the overcast day. Even though it is only 60 degrees and the skies are overcast, the outside would seem warm and bright after just a few minutes in the black, cold cave. They squint in the daylight and regroup near the entrance.

They must talk about the cave's smell, what they've seen inside. If any of them smoke, maybe they have a cigarette while they contemplate re-entering the cave or going home. Eventually the lure of the black space wins.

While they sit outside the cave and consider their next step, their lungs re-acclimate to normal air. If they had any early symptoms of carbon monoxide poisoning, the effects might evaporate after they breathe the improved air. But they would still have some elevated levels of carbon monoxide in their systems. And some of the first effects of carbon monoxide poisoning would begin to impede the ability to make clear decisions and sound judgments.

The five teens re-enter the cave, most likely pushing beyond their first exploration. But they retrace their steps a second time, retreating outside the cave opening. Here they might again recover slightly, though their blood levels of carbon monoxide are even higher. Perhaps they contemplate leaving. Ultimately, they go back in, farther than either of their two previous explorations.

At about 3:45 PM, St. Paul police officers Anthony T. Spencer and Genaro Valentin, Squad 228, are dispatched to the Minnesota Department of Agriculture building. Someone has called to report teenagers entering the caves on the West Side bluff. Dispatch informs the officers "the report is second hand information reported through the Parks and Rec Department. The information was not specific as to location other than behind 90 W. Plato Blvd."

Valentin and Spencer nose their cruiser into the Department of Agriculture's spacious parking lot. They cruise down its length and scan the lot for anyone or anything suspicious.

Nothing appears to be out of place. Two people move toward their cars. The officers ask, but neither person made the call to the Parks and Rec Department. And have they seen anyone in the snarl of wild growth behind the building, messing along the bluff? Neither person has seen anyone. The officers' report continues,

Officer Valentin and I have worked the West Side for the past four years and are familiar with the cave system that runs along the bluff south of Plato Blvd. We have responded to calls recently involving fires in the caves. We have been advised by the Fire Dept on several occasions involving fires in the caves that they would not respond unless we knew of people in the caves, because it was too dangerous to send rescue personnel in. We were aware of ventilation holes in this particular area of the bluff, but we were not familiar with any points of ingress or egress to the caves from this general area. We were aware of additional ventilation holes east of the Agriculture building along the bluff behind the Health Partners building. We checked this location and again did not locate anything that appeared to be unusual or out of place. We did not observe any smoke in the area along the bluff line or anything else that would have led us to believe persons were in the caves. After clearing the call, GOA [Gone On Arrival] we checked the area of the bluff line to the west of the Agriculture building again not observing anything that appeared to be out of the ordinary. There were still numerous vehicles in the parking lots of the businesses along W. Plato Blvd. So none of the vehicles stood out as appearing out of place. When Officer Valentin and I worked Tour III (1600–0200) it would be common to find randomly parked vehicles near the bluff line that would belong to people exploring the cave system. We did not observe any vehicles that appeared to not belong in the area due to the large amount of vehicles parked in the area for the business day.

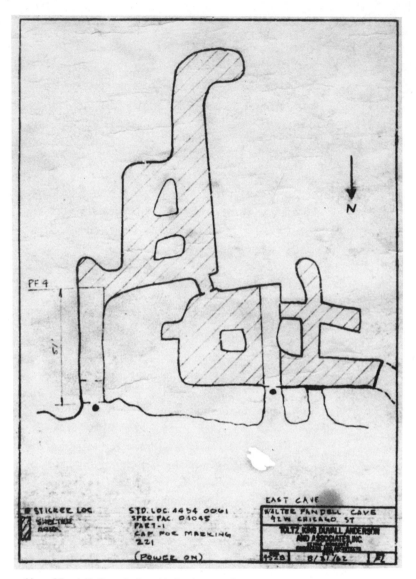

Map of Fandell's Cave, believed to be the cave the teens entered. Courtesy Greg Brick

The officers declare the location clear and continue to monitor radio traffic.

The cave isn't a single straight tunnel stretching far back into the cliff. It zigzags. After the three-foot rise and climb through the low-hung large space with the pillar, a small tunnel leads from the back of the room. It is difficult to climb through but traversable—a six-foot drop through a rabbit hole with debris to make it interesting. Then the room at the bottom opens up into another cavernous space with more turns and side tunnels and debris spread out over the sandy floor. There are places where the corridor narrows or the teens have to make a turn around a large cave pillar or they make another turn into a tunnel that dead ends. And there is lots of junk in the cave, some of it so large they have to climb over the debris or scoot around or under it.

Near the end of their third entry into the cave, they are as far back as they have ever been. Jay and Natalie crawl on all fours through a narrow opening. When they push into the next room, they both smell a chemical-like smoke that makes it harder to breathe. They call through the narrow opening to the others, telling them not to enter. And they retreat back through the space, trying to get away from the fumes.

Here Natalie, presumably the group's lightest explorer, with the least amount of body mass to absorb the poisonous gas, begins to falter. She complains of feeling light-headed, dizzy, not right. Jay notices the others are having trouble breathing and standing up. When Natalie stumbles in the dark, unable to maintain her equilibrium, beginning to pass out, Jay and Justin are close enough to assist. They begin to help her exit the cave.

By now they're deep inside the old sandstone mine. Informal mappings of this cave put its overall depth at approximately a hundred feet; several news accounts later report that they are six hundred feet, two-thirds of a football field, inside the cave. Perhaps the tunnel's twists and turns add to the length. By now Justin and Jay are feeling the effects of carbon monoxide poisoning. With more body weight than Natalie, they have been able to maintain at least some level of consciousness while their companions stumble and finally pass out. Jay and Justin carry Natalie a few feet before the effects of the gas start taking their toll, making them weak, dizzy, and disoriented. *If* they have a lucid thought, it is the understanding that something is terribly wrong, that they have to get out of the cave, they have to escape to sunlight. In the jumbled confusion, they hear calls for help from their friends and then nothing. They no longer have the ability to make clear decisions. They stumble in the dark.

And then Justin falls.

Jay struggles with the unconscious Natalie. But as anyone who has ever tried to pick up and carry an adult can attest, it is an enormous weight. And then he, too, falters and drops.

Fate's single saving moment occurs sometime over the next minute or two, while Jay Boucher lies on the ground in the cave. He may have fallen near the front of the cave, near a place with a little more oxygen than in other parts of the cave. Jay wakes up. Not completely, not coherently, but enough to move forward. He finds his flashlight on the ground and stumbles through the cave, disoriented, searching for any kind of landmark or familiar feature in the dark. He cannot find his friends. He cannot see their lights or any sign of them. His only thought is to get out of that space. His beam passes across the wall, and he reads "Tom loves Lisa," familiar graffiti he noticed on the way in. He sees a patch of light and moves toward it, crawling up the last hilly rise of sand. He manages to get out of the cave, knows he has to go for help. But it is a fleeting thought. He is dizzy, disoriented; he does not really know what's happening. He knows something is very, very wrong. Very terribly wrong. His friends are all behind, still inside the cave. He sits down to try to clear his head. He doesn't know how long he sits.

Maybe he turns and yells back into the opening, calling his friends by name. But there is nothing, only the empty echo off the black chamber into which his voice finally fades.

After what might be fifteen minutes in the light, Jay rights himself and lurches like a drunk down the forested hillside.

Behind the Department of Agriculture building, there are no open, unlocked entrances. The windows are tinted, and there is no apparent place to turn for help. He stumbles down the hillside, along the back of the building, not thinking clearly but remembering he has to go for help, he must turn to someone for help. He staggers down the length of bluff path, returning to their car in the HealthPartners parking lot. He has to find someone. Someone for help. Someone to call. But he doesn't know. He doesn't know what's happening, what happened, what happened to his friends. He steps over the lot, still disoriented.

And then a HealthPartners employee, a woman just getting off work and walking toward her car, notices the boy. He is obviously struggling. He obviously needs assistance. Perhaps at first she wonders about it, but a second look and maybe a raised plea for assistance or a glance at Jay Boucher's frightened eyes convinces her to come to his aid.

And in a moment the woman learns there are still kids in one of the caves up the hillside. And that something has gone terribly wrong. She dials 911. It is 4:21 PM.

7

Rescue and Recovery
City fire stations and the West Side bluffs, St. Paul
Tuesday, April 27, 2004, 4:21 pm

The 911 call comes into central dispatch, and the woman describes Jay Boucher's troubling condition and his account of kids trapped in the West Side caves. The dispatcher routes the call to Fire and Emergency Medical Services. The fire dispatcher determines which resources should be activated, then sends out the call to Fire District 2—which covers the middle third of St. Paul—and tells Engines 1, 8, and 15, Ladder 8, Squad 1, and Fire District Chief Marty Ludden to respond.

This all happens in a matter of seconds. Time is precious, especially for the teenagers who have been in and out of the caves for over an hour.

Engine 15 is located on the corner of Caesar Chavez and Isabel streets, about two long city blocks from 205 South Wabasha Street. Suddenly the station is filled with alarm tones and lights and a blasting voice over the public address system. As Fire Captain Bill Lee, Firefighter Geno Flores, and Fire Equipment Operator Mike Newbauer race toward their equipment and truck, dispatch tells the entire district it is a code red, there are people trapped in the caves, and the person making the call is in the parking lot at 205 South Wabasha. In seconds, firefighters are on their rig and blasting out of the station, lights and sirens blaring.

Newbauer drives and Lee and Flores suit up en route. They pull into the HealthPartners lot just after 4:22, ninety seconds after the 911 call came in. A woman near the back of the lot flags down their truck, and Jay Boucher comes forward.

Boucher manages to tell them the opening to the cave is behind 90 West Plato Boulevard, the Department of Agriculture building. Newbauer barely pauses as they hustle Boucher onto the truck and wheel down the long block to the building on Plato. They pull into the lot and park near the building's front right corner. Boucher thinks there are three or four kids in the cave . . . that something is wrong. They passed out. He managed to stumble toward the light, toward escape, but he doesn't know what happened. He doesn't know if anyone else made it out. He is clearly distraught and not altogether coherent.

Captain Lee, who grew up in St. Paul, sometimes crawled through the large complexes with his friends when he was a kid. He knows they can be treacherous, tight places, but most often they are explored by the city's youth without encountering anything more than skinned knees and a little adventure.

During the first three weeks in April, Captain Lee and other firefighters had responded to the calls regarding smoke in the caves. But the smoldering cave fires were closer to Wabasha, farther east along the bluff from 90 West Plato Boulevard. So he knows these kids didn't walk into a fire. Something else must be wrong.

When the emergency tones start blaring and the lights come on, Second District Chief Ludden is working at his desk in Fire Station 8, on the corner of Tenth and Minnesota Streets. He is across the Mississippi, at least a mile from 90 West Plato Boulevard. He listens to the PA announce the code red, that people are in the caves, the location, and the engines to respond—one of them from his station. There is a GPS in the district chief's truck, but he certainly doesn't need it. In seconds the six-foot-four, white-haired, athletic Ludden is down the pole to the apparatus floor where the rigs and the chief's truck sit ready. He climbs into the red Chevy Suburban, hits the roof lights and sirens, and pushes it out of the station. The Suburban holds his gear (fire-protective clothing and an air pack), spare equipment for fire fighters, floor plans and maps, department forms, radios, a computer, and water for the crews on the scene. The Suburban's light bar includes an

OptiCom—a strobe that changes traffic control lights. The OptiCom opens a path so District Chief Ludden can roar across the tight, traffic-filled city streets. It takes him longer to respond than Engine 15, but not by much.

On the scene, Ludden knows he will have a *full assignment,* standard in a response to a structure fire or something like a cave rescue. A full assignment includes three engines (for this event, Engines 1, 8, and 15), one truck or ladder (Ladder 8), and one squad (Squad 1).

There are three squads located at strategic points throughout the city. They carry extra manpower, spare air bottles including some breathing tanks that last an entire hour, heavy rescue equipment, generators and lights with cord reels, and hazmat (hazardous materials) response gear. The squads are specially trained, and their skill set includes confined space rescue.

On the way over, Fire District Chief Ludden worries about his men inside those caves. The old sandstone mines are confined spaces with unknown hazards. He radios everyone responding to stand down until they know for certain what they are addressing and what kind of equipment is best suited for going into those caves.

As Lee and Flores get out of the truck and race around the building toward the cave entrance, they hear the chief's order: "Don't enter that cave until we know what we're getting into."

Bill Lee is used to taking orders, but he is also used to making his own decisions. He and Flores pause. Time is precious. If those other kids are near the entrance, they'll need to get them out fast. The captain and firefighter Flores continue up the hillside toward the narrow, dark entrance.

Lee doesn't think about violating orders. He thinks about saving some kids. They find the narrow cave maw exactly where Jay Boucher said it would be in the steep thicketed hillside, and the two barely pause before they slide one at a time through the black opening, flashlights in hand, their beams cutting the murky darkness. Five feet down the sandy slope they can stand up in the eerie darkness.

"Hello! Hey! Anyone? Anyone there?"

Their calls echo back unanswered.

They peer into the dark and wait long enough for their eyes to adjust and then begin their hurried, shadowy exploration.

As Ludden pulls onto Plato, he sees Engines 15 and 1 already present, just down the street at the Department of Agriculture building. The firefighters from Engine 1 have just arrived and are starting to prepare for a cave entry, awaiting the chief's directions. Fire Equipment Operator Newbauer has moved up near the cave entrance. Lee and Flores are already in the cave.

Ludden parks his red Suburban and watches an unsteady, distraught Jay Boucher approach the truck. It is 4:24, three minutes since the 911 call came in.

In the darkness, the compact, muscular Flores and Captain Lee see a short passage to their right, a passage in front of them, and one to their left. Flores checks out the space to his right. After about ten or fifteen feet, it stops at a blank wall.

"Dead end," he reports. Then they both move into the passageway in front of them.

Lee turns and repeats his call into the darkness. "Anyone! Anyone there?" But again, no answer.

The two move forward. After about forty feet the cave has an intersection, and they hurriedly step into both sides. But these short passages are also dead ends. They move forward another thirty feet and reach another rubble-filled dead end. They retrace the seventy feet back to the entrance and finally look into the only other way open to them, a passage to the left.

The two move carefully and quickly into the debris-filled space. Ten feet forward, they climb over a three-foot brick wall. They slant right into a wide cavern with a huge center pillar. Here the ceiling is only four feet tall, and they have to crouch as they circle through the rubble-filled room. Lee bends down and steps right while Flores bends and continues toward the left wall.

The walls are covered with graffiti, and the sand floor is littered with remnants of brick and rubble. They have to step carefully, but quickly. Flores circles the large central pillar and meets Lee from the other side.

"Anything?" Lee asks.

"Nothing." Flores shakes his head.

Neither of them has seen or found any sign of the kids. And their calls into the murky darkness fade into silence. They wonder if they are in the right cave. This was the only cave entrance they could see along the bluff, but there doesn't appear to be anyone in it. They head back to the entrance, clamber up the sandy slope, and squeeze out the narrow opening, squinting into the daylight.

Jay Boucher is coherent enough to tell Marty Ludden what he told the others. There are three (four?) kids still in the caves, passed out. He manages to draw Ludden a simple map.

One of the firefighters from Squad 1 has taken carbon

monoxide readings at the cave entrance. His meter registers 70 PPM, higher than OSHA recommendations, but at those levels it would take a long time to be deadly. They don't know the carbon monoxide level in the far reaches of the cave.

The firefighters return to their rigs and report the carbon monoxide readings to Ludden. He immediately orders everyone to use their self-contained breathing apparatus (SCBA) and full protective gear. Firefighters Geno Flores, Danny Fronk, Scott Sletten, and Troy Teff all don the tanks and take two three-hundred-foot guide ropes and related gear up with them to the entrance. Under normal conditions, the tanks should provide one half hour of air. These are anything but normal conditions.

Lee and Flores describe the cave's twists and turns and rubble. It's like an obstacle course, and they didn't see anyone, but there are nooks and crannies all over the place. The firefighters hope they can use the guide ropes to lay down a trail system.

Fully suited, they head back to the cave opening.

The entrance is so tight they cannot climb through it wearing their tanks. First they slide, one at a time, through the narrow opening and then reach back to pull their tanks in after them. Once inside and down the sandy slope, there is an open place to stand and gear up. There are now around six firefighters at the bottom of the entrance, starting to move into the cave. Flores wears a SCBA tank, but Lee didn't want to be encumbered with it. The tank, suit, and related gear can weigh over fifty pounds, making an already troubling walk, bend, and crawl through the debris-laden space even more difficult. And Lee has already ruptured one disk in his firefighting career. His lower back strains with the effort of the low crawl and bend through the passages. But he and Flores need to show the others where they searched. They guide the small team over the three-foot wall and into the wide room with a central pillar and low ceiling.

Some of the team have carbon monoxide monitors, and once inside the large cavern they discover levels of carbon monoxide over 100 PPM, with oxygen levels at 15 percent. Twenty-one percent is normal.

They call out the readings in the room. "Getting dangerous," one of them comments.

Lee starts back along the low-hung passage.

Their tanks have one half hour of air. To stay in here without good air is to risk unconsciousness, which is probably why none of the teenagers in this underground maze—if this is the right cave—is answering their calls. By now the firefighters begin to fear the worst. With the carbon monoxide levels rising as they get farther into this maze, they know it is becoming a death trap. The teenagers made their first entry over an hour earlier. None of the firefighters mentions their fears. They continue moving as rapidly as possible through the troubling terrain.

They take another turn around the thick central pillar, their flashlights flickering through the dark. Along the rear wall, they discover a small dark hole. When they shine their lights into the narrow space, it appears to tunnel down and then open into another room, like a big rabbit hole into a large warren. And from the marks along the sand floor, it looks like the passage has been recently traversed.

At this point Flores waits at the entrance to the hole while Fronk, Sletten, and Teff make the difficult slide and crawl through the narrow hole. The tunnel is a tight, debris-filled space with some old steel rebar and broken bricks complicating their passage. But after a few feet, the firefighters enter another section of spacious cave and they can all stand up. The cave spreads out and back to the left, and there is another pillar and even more debris.

Over the next fifteen minutes, the firefighters lay down rope and take turns searching through the maze of rubble-filled passages and cavernous spaces. They know every second counts. But the place is a catacomb, and sections are filled nearly to the ceiling with steel rebar and old construction waste. Other passages are low crawls over twisted metal and junk. It is like a diabolical obstacle course in a maze with no map. And the extra pounds of tank and related equipment and the suits make it all the more difficult to traverse. And as they move deeper into the bluff cave passages, the figures on their monitors continue to climb. At one point, a few hundred feet into the cave, they register levels upward of 600 PPM, marking an extremely lethal space. The aerobic effort required to bend, climb, crawl, and push through sand to get this far into the cave forces the firefighters to run through their half-hour tanks faster than normal. After several minutes exploring the back reaches of this new section of cave, they have to turn back. But they are pretty sure this is the way. There is more cave and more passage in front of them that will have to be explored by another team, preferably wearing one-hour tanks.

This deep into the cave, their radios cannot reach out to the surface. They have to relay their messages through Flores, waiting back at the rabbit hole entrance. They tell him they are heading out, they are running out of air. They also tell the next team, waiting near the entrance, to use one-hour tanks. It is a deep, difficult crawl of several hundred feet through climbing carbon monoxide levels. They will need every breath of clean air they have.

On their way out, they meet a second team coming in. Captain Mike Scheller and firefighter Jerry Simon enter the cave. Flores and Teff exchange their expended half-hour tanks for one-hour tanks and head back through the passages with Scheller and Simon. They make their way to the rabbit hole. By now a rope and extra lights guide them along the right route, but it is still a difficult walk, bend, and crawl. Near the narrow entrance Scheller waits while Teff, Simon, and Flores climb down the narrow tunnel into the spacious rear cavern. They pick up the search where the previous team left off, and finally, after at least fifteen minutes of a difficult crawl into the far reaches of this cave, the room begins to narrow again. There is a tunnel at the end of it. Flores has gone off to search another quarter of the dark region. Teff and Simon move toward the narrowing tunnel. It is very tight and angles down at a gradual slant. But it looks like there is space at the bottom that opens up. Maybe another chamber.

Jerry Simon crawls into the tight space and with considerable effort makes it down the incline. At the bottom, in front of a large mound of sand and debris, he finds the first victim. It is a young man. He is small—or perhaps he appears small, lying prone and lifeless on the narrow floor.

"Found one of them!" Simon screams back to Teff through his mask.

Simon's quick examination reveals no pulse and no breath. This deep in the bluff, their radios remain useless. Teff crawls down the passage and together they manage to extract him from the distant chamber. Perhaps if they can get him out quickly enough there may still be a chance. But it is very far back and by now the boy has been in these lethal environs for a long time and the way back is incredibly difficult, even *without* carrying an unconscious body. They hustle back up the chute with their burden, pushing and pulling, hoping for the best, fearing the worst.

Finally they near the forward hole with Captain Scheller at the top, and they let him know they've found one, a boy, but he is not breathing. Flores is there to assist, and the three struggle back up through the tunnel with their terrible burden.

They did not see any other kids, but now they know the vicinity of the first victim, and they could see, at the bottom of that distant tunnel, up over the hummock of sand and debris, a deeper chamber that opened up.

By now Alan Gabriele and Germaine Mitchell have also put on one-hour breathing tanks and are into the cave, following the rope trail as far as it leads. They pass Scheller and Teff, Simon and Flores, struggling with the first victim. They crawl down into the first rabbit hole and follow the rope all the way to its end. At the end of the rope there is a kind of fork, and they turn right, following the greatest number of tracks in the sand. They keep hurrying forward through the tight, difficult quarters. Finally they come to the narrowing tunnel, and to get down through it Alan Gabriele has to take off his tank. He carefully pulls it after him, and once at the bottom he re-shoulders it. He checks his monitor, and the reading is over 700 PPM.

Finally he manages to climb up the sandy debris hill just beyond the bottom of the chute, and there, in a kind of wide chamber, he finds the other victims. It takes him a moment to climb over the hill and into the space. The first victim is prone on the low floor with no pulse or breath. There is a girl who appears to have crawled a short way into a side chamber. She, too, has no pulse or breath. And in the center of the room, on a slightly elevated stone slab, lies another victim.

It is an eerie scene. It looks to Gabriele like a remote, primitive party room, like maybe the kids had come back here to have a little fun. But then the deadly gas overtook them, and now they lie in the postures in which they took their final breaths.

Germaine Mitchell has crawled down the chute to come in behind him. Together they begin checking the victims and trying to figure out how they are going to extract them from this deep space, over eight hundred feet underground through one of the most difficult, troubling crawls either has ever made.

And then Alan Gabriele notices that the kid in the center of the room appears to be taking difficult, short, almost imperceptible breaths. Gabriele moves forward to have a closer look. The kid is unconscious but definitely struggling to breathe.

"This one's still breathing," he exclaims.

Mitchell and Gabriele cannot waste a moment. They relay the message out and turn to their arduous task. Their SCBA tanks will likely run out of air before they reach the front entrance, but they expend every effort to get the boy up the narrow chute and down back along the narrowing tunnel and through the passageway and the cavernous room. Another team has entered the cave with a skid stretcher, and after they get the victim up out of the first rabbit hole they can put him on the stretcher and hurry through the four-foot-high space, as fast as physically possible, and finally they turn the corner and reach the mound of sand and they scrabble up the mound and out with the skid sled and the boy is rushed to a waiting EMS team, who begin administering oxygen while their sirens scream and they speed toward Hennepin County Medical Center. This one has a very faint pulse and is barely breathing. This one they may be able to save.

The first team brings out the first of four people at 5:09, forty-eight minutes after the 911 call came in. By the time the kid who is still breathing gets extracted, it is later. A third victim, Natalie VanVorst, is brought out by another team.

Captain Mike Selander is outside the cave, suiting up to take his team in and recover the last victim. He watches them bring out the girl on a skid sled. He glances at her, to see if he might know her. He has a daughter himself, though she is older now. There were plenty of nights when she was the age of this girl and he and his wife worried about her. Not that she needed to be worried about, but the anxiety of seeing your children through their teenage years is simply part of the process.

He looks at the girl but doesn't recognize her. As the fire-fighters help haul the girl down the hillside, everyone grows quiet, solemn, reverential. No one can speak as they carry the victim down the hillside to the waiting EMS.

Not long after the 911 call, more than one EMS truck is on the scene along with the fire engines. It has not taken long for the media to respond to the rescue and recovery. By the time the firefighters bring out the first person on the sled, the bluff and outside building and parking lot are packed with police, firefighters, EMS personnel, reporters with cameras, and bystanders.

* * *

After a brief wait outside, Captain Mike Selander and fire-fighters Tom Hickey, Kate Michalski, and Dan Newton put on their tanks and head into the cave. Selander is forty-eight years old, five feet nine inches, and two hundred pounds. Over his career he has been in plenty of tight places and never had a problem. But something about this entry makes him edgy. First he has to get down and set his tank on the mound in front of the narrow black opening. Then he has to slide feetfirst through the gap, bringing his tank down after him. Once inside the narrow tunnel, his pulse suddenly spikes. He cannot see the bottom and he becomes, for the first time in his life, claustrophobic. It is a tight crawl, something he has executed before without any difficulty. But for some reason this time he *feels* the tightness of the space, and it unnerves him. He recognizes it and at the same time recognizes his responsibility to his team, the other three firefighters following him in. Selander chokes back his fear and suits up as his team members come in behind him and do the same. Then they are off, following the ropes and lights through the labyrinth. They find the rabbit hole at the back of the low-hung cavern, they climb down into it, and they follow the rope farther into the deep, cavernous stretches.

Finally, they come to the end of six hundred feet and there is no clear sign which way to turn. At this point there is a kind of fork. To the left, the sandy floor trails off into the dark. To the right, another passage disappears into darkness. Selander sees more tracks in the sand to the right, so he takes the more traveled path.

Walking along the sandy floor makes the traverse this deep into the cave difficult. It is like walking along a rubble-filled beach. Every step sinks and slides back and slows their momentum. They cannot get a good grip on this floor, and it adds to their labor.

Selander's team is wearing half-hour tanks, and Selander has had to work so hard his tank is low. But by now other firefighters have ferried in caches of full air tanks. Hickey, Michalski, and Newton are all younger firefighters. All of them do a lot of aerobic training, and it shows. Even this far back into the cave, they move more easily and with less breath and effort.

Finally, they make it to the narrowing tunnel and crawl down the passage and make it up over the sandy hill into the deadly chamber and find the last victim, a boy. They get the boy up out of the tunnel and put him on a skid sled and begin hauling him back over the space they just crossed. Selander's SCBA starts beeping, a sign his tank is nearly empty. Up ahead he finds one of the caches and swaps out his tank for a fresh one, and they continue.

Over the next half hour, the only good news comes from one of the ambulances on the scene, relaying reports on seventeen-year-old Justin Jensen. They managed to keep him breathing, and he is being treated in the hyperbaric chamber at Hennepin County Medical Center. Hyperbaric oxygen treatment involves the use of pressurized oxygen to help heal tissues damaged by carbon monoxide poisoning and other infections or injuries.

The rescue and recovery continues for almost another hour. Finally, by 6:20, Selander and his team bring the last body out of the cave.

8
Aftermath
Twin Cities southern suburbs and St. Paul
April 27, 2004, and the days and months following

The hours and days immediately after the five students' entry into St. Paul's West Side caves are filled with the care of the two survivors, the treatment of some of the firefighters, and the difficult, terrible effort to come to terms with the fact that some did not come out alive.

Jay Boucher is treated at a nearby hospital and released later in the day.

Captain Bill Lee and firefighter Geno Flores are ordered to report to the hospital for evaluation. Lee has elevated levels of carbon monoxide in his system. He is treated with oxygen, and both are released that same day.

Justin Jensen's treatment in the hyperbaric chamber enables him to make a dramatic and complete recovery in just one day. He is released from the hospital on April 28.

The families, students, and staff of Cedar Alternative School, and people throughout the Twin Cities metropolitan area and the country, are stunned by the news of the deaths of Natalie VanVorst, Nick Larson, and Patrick Dague. Markers and memorials left at the cave entrance and along the bluff behind the Department of Agriculture building are a small reflection of the devastating loss of three young lives. The victims are memorialized in heavily attended funeral services.

In the longer term, the authorities begin the complex task of addressing the tragic lessons learned from the event. The city of St. Paul hires CNA Consulting Engineers to survey and map the caves along the entire length of the West Side bluff. From September 27 to October 4 the survey is conducted, with the help of several firefighters, at a cost of $11,000. They discover the caves are so numerous, complex, and deep it would be virtually impossible to fill them. In the 1980s, filling one of the largest caverns required 6,500 truckloads of construction debris.

The consulting firm finds eighty-one cave entrances in the bluff, thirty-seven of them in the downstream and more populated end. Fandell's Cave, where the teens entered the bluff, is in the middle of the lower segment. The firm recommends the entrances be dug out and filled in with class-five construction materials (recycled concrete, soil, or rocks) at an estimated cost of $1 million. The city struggles to come up with the funds, ultimately taking a slower approach to sealing the caves. It begins by posting signs. Orange, laminated, light cardboard notices are affixed to survey sticks and staked into the ground at frequent intervals along the bluff. The signs read,

NO TRESPASSING
Unauthorized access to this park property is prohibited
Violators will be prosecuted
This area is under surveillance and routine patrol
City of St. Paul
Department of Parks and Recreation
Parkwatch: 651-646-3535

The city continues to search for the funds required to permanently seal the entrances. Meanwhile, they periodically police the bluffs.

On April 27, 2005, exactly one year after the tragic cave fatalities, the *Star Tribune* carries an article entitled, "A year after trio died, no answer on caves, St. Paul still needs funds to permanently seal entrances."

The St. Paul Parks Department successfully seals some of the caves, including the one the teenagers entered on April 27, 2004. But others remain open.

Just four years after the entrance to Fandell's Cave was sealed over with large pieces of limestone and sand, the trail along the bluffs is clearly open and being used. People, probably kids and vagrants, have been hiking along the base of the bluff behind the trees. The path is no wider than a deer trail, and part of it meanders less than five feet from the blocked entry to Fandell's. Unfortunately, there are signs of fresh digging around the entrance, possibly by a new generation of amateur explorers who are anxious for a little adventure and wholly unfamiliar with the potentially lethal dangers of penetrating the subterranean unknown.

PART THREE
Opening Goliath
Wild cave near Spring Valley, Southeastern Minnesota,
  1980–2008

9
Discovery
Jessie's Grove, Southeastern Minnesota
Sunday, September 21, 1980, approximately 5:00 pm

Ron Spong pulls his old Ford van to the side of the gravel road. He lets the dust settle before he rolls down the window to get some air. It is a beautiful afternoon, with a partly cloudy sky and air freshened by two nights of rain. Spong, raised on a farm north of Rochester, Minnesota, likes to be outside. After a long day's work mapping southeastern Minnesota's karst features and bedrock geology, he has decided to reward himself with one more effort to push into the far reaches of a wild cave.

It isn't the typical end to a workday. Many thirty-seven-year-olds might sidle up to a dark wooden bar and order themselves something frosty. But ever since the ninth grade, when he read some nonfiction books on caving for an English class, Spong has been intrigued by the subterranean world.

Soon after the English project, some friends told him about a cave that needed exploring near Hammond, Minnesota, and he gladly joined in, not realizing it would lead to a lifelong fascination with caves. In May 1962 he would be a founding member of the Minnesota Speleological Survey, which eventually became a local grotto, or state chapter, of the National Speleological Society. And in 1976 he would found the Minnesota Institute of Speleology, a specialized organization whose small membership is devoted to the exploration, mapping, and documentation of caves.

This afternoon he cuts the engine on his old Ford van and climbs in back, starting to change into his coveralls. At six feet five inches and 220 pounds, he has a harder time squeezing through caves than most cavers. His caving outfit consists of farm coveralls, a hard hat, a Justrite electric headlamp, gloves, and boots. He gathers his side pack and safety gear, including a medium flashlight, a small waterproof flashlight, and a candle and waterproof matches for backup. When he began cave exploring in the late 1950s, some of his outfit was vintage World War II and Korean War equipment from an army-navy surplus store. Through the intervening years, he upgraded his caving gear for safety and even cosmetic reasons.

After gearing up, he locks the van and starts hiking through several hundred yards of fallow field toward the thick, tree-lined boundary of Jessie's Grove. The pungent odors of witch hazel and fading green seedpods fill the late afternoon air.

Spong has been prospecting open places in the earth in Minnesota's karst region since he was fourteen, and today he is going to see if he can get lucky. Johnny Johnson, Pete Cramer, George Buisse, and some of the other old-timers from the commercial Niagara Cave had probably been in this one before, in the mid-1950s. Johnny Johnson had whetted his appetite by telling him there was over a thousand feet of wild cave in there, probably more, providing you can get into it.

The dark crevice the old-timers named Coon Cave is a wet cave. Sometimes the wild entrance is covered over. Floodwaters from a good rain can easily fill the cave with debris and talus or scree- -large chunks of limestone the weather has worked away from the bedrock. In fact, not long after the Niagara cavers discovered and named Coon Cave, a flood caused a massive collapse of rock and other debris, and the only entrance to the cave was sealed solid.

For the next twenty-five years, Spong and like-minded caving enthusiasts tried to dig the entrance open by hand, but there was just too much heavy, choking fill. Then on May 26—this year's Memorial Day—the skies opened and dropped seven inches of rain on the area. The square of dense woodland has sinkholes and a blind valley along with the natural entrance to this wild cave. Over Memorial Day the place was underwater.

The hydro-power of heavy rain can be enigmatic. The same whimsy that once solidly sealed this cave suddenly opened it. Not long after, Spong happened to check on the old entrance and realized that with a little digging it could be re-opened and explored.

And that is just what he and his caving buddies Rick Cunningham and Ted Marshall did. They made several June trips into the cave, and they were intrigued by what they found. Unfortunately, after crawling and stooping through some excellent, pretty open cave passages for two hundred feet, some of it through a flowing underground streambed, they discovered a large sump on the first trip. Sumps are submerged passages, low places where water pools and the cave roof comes down to meet it. While Spong and his friends generally use wet suits to traverse sumps, they plan those expeditions rarely. On a later trip, they did get beyond it without wet suits, crawling on their bellies through ice-cold water and pushing to the other side. And then, after another thirty feet of open cave passage, they found another sump. This second one was a little narrower, a little deeper, and a little more difficult to penetrate. They were unable to move beyond it.

But Spong remembers what Johnny Johnson told him. Beyond the second sump there is all that wild, largely un-explored cave, probably much more than a thousand feet. Cunningham and Marshall and Spong think the old-timers are right, because when they stood at a narrow crevice near the first sump, they could feel air on the backs of their heads, blowing into the cave.

Spong has a theory about this cave. Johnson and the Niagara cavers did not have wet suits. At some point the sumps must become dry enough to traverse without them. And Spong has a hunch, since there are other small caves in the area, that what lies beyond that second sump could open into a major section of wild cave. He wants to find out for himself the veracity of the old-timers' claims.

Spong enjoys his walk through the autumn field. It is warm in the late afternoon, and he slants toward the edge of thick trees with a happy squint in his eyes.

While he feels good about having another look at Coon Cave, he is also a little reluctant. One of the first things he tells any young caver is to never, *never* go in alone. Spong has plenty of obligations—his wife Katie and their four children, ages twelve, eleven, seven, and one, to name five of the most important. He is a little concerned about his lone probe. But he tells himself at least he did the next best thing. He asked permission of the farmer who rents the land and said that he would let the farmer know when he was out safely. If he doesn't make it back, the farmer knows whom to contact.

Spong approaches the line of trees with his gear rattling beside him. The big boots and coveralls make walking through the tall prairie grass awkward. And the push through the field warms him. He's looking forward to entering the coolness of the cave.

Jessie's Grove, the twenty-five-acre tract where the natural entrance to the cave sinks into the earth, is heavily wooded. Walk around for five minutes, and you realize why it was never clear-cut and farmed. An old creek bed—Jessie's Kill—runs through it, with sinkholes and, in places, trees and understory so thick it is practically impassable. It is one of those geologic oddities called a *blind valley:* when Jessie's Kill fills with water, the creek flows into the woods and disappears.

Between 1976 and 1980, Spong performed several fluorescent dye traces of water sinking in Jessie's Grove and in the

Canfield Creek valley to the east. He watched the bright green dye disappear into the ground and reappear two to three days later nearly three miles away at Canfield Big (Trout) Spring, in the lower reach of Canfield Creek. Where there is an underground river of that length, there is very likely an extensive cave system.

Spong crosses into the thick woods, parting branches with his gloved hand and pushing several hundred yards through dense undergrowth to the edge of the pit where the cave entrance lies. Jessie's Kill has overwhelmed two of the area's known sinkholes, Downwater Sink and Woebegone Sink, indicating the runoff from the rain of the past two nights is still making its way into the grove.

Unless you are right on top of the eastern edge of Coon Cave's natural amphitheater entrance, where the limestone cliff drops off ten to twenty feet as though the face of the pit were a stone retaining wall, you wouldn't see the opening. The amphitheater is at least thirty feet across, but the way it drops away from the tree- and brush-covered surface makes it almost impossible to find.

Spong circles around from the western edge until he is standing at the top of the limestone wall. The cave entrance, a flat, broad, five-by-three-foot black hole down and across the pit, still looks clear and open. On June 28, the last time they entered the cave, Marshall, Cunningham, and Spong surveyed the cave with a measuring tape and a Brunton compass, which allows the measurement of inclines. They named the different parts of the first 270 feet of cave. Once inside, he will cross over the Talus Fell and move another forty to fifty feet to Hourglass Pass, where he will crawl and stoop-walk down the streambed that often has water running through it. From there he will pass by Slaughter Canyon and enter the Echo Lake Gallery. When the water is high, this passage is filled with water and the acoustics form a powerful echo in the wide, high passage. The Echo Lake Gallery has two sumps, Echo-1 and Echo-2. The Echo-1 Sump is wide and low. The Echo-2 Sump is narrower and higher. Sometimes cavers describe sumps like these as *water traps*. If you get to the other side and the water rises, the sump could close, effectively sealing you in an underground tomb.

Spong descends the twenty-foot cliff with the help of some natural protruding limestone ledges—like steep stair steps. At the gaping cave maw, he affixes his helmet and makes sure his Justrite lamp with its fresh D batteries is on. He also has backup batteries and the small hand flashlights. He expects

The natural entrance to Goliath's Cave. Courtesy John Ackerman

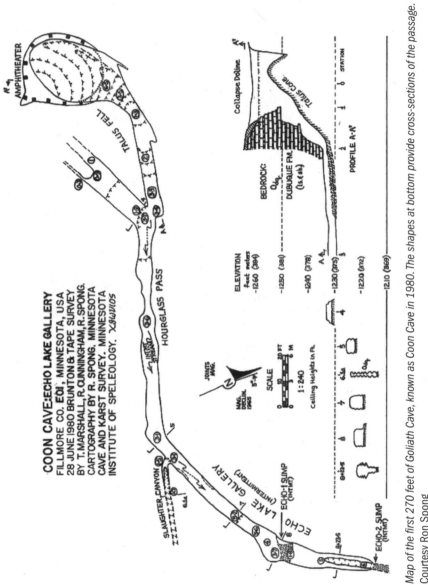

Map of the first 270 feet of Goliath Cave, known as Coon Cave in 1980. The shapes at bottom provide cross-sections of the passage.
Courtesy Ron Spong

there will be water, and he wishes he'd brought along his wet suit, mask, and snorkel—the only way to properly pass the Echo Lake Gallery and Echo-1 Sump.

The few wet cavers with nerve enough to push near-sumps, in which the floor is flooded almost to the ceiling, refer to the technique as *blowing bubbles*. The explorer lies on his back with his mouth pressed to the ceiling, gulping in precious air from a tiny air space. Sometimes his movement through the sump generates waves that momentarily block the space, forcing the explorer to blow bubbles through his nose to keep the water out until the wave passes, the space reopens, and he can breathe again. Spong has done it before, and he will do it again. But the already dangerous technique is less problematic when he is using the right equipment.

Unfortunately, he didn't really plan this visit. The idea of visiting Coon Cave surfaced as an idle thought during the weekend and then gained a little strength, until today he thought it might be worth a try. He had come back alone on July 20 to check out the cave, but the second sump had been impassable. And now observing all the surface water that has filled Woebegone and Downwater sinks makes him feel edgy. The rising water is a potentially dangerous sign. And while he has plenty of light, he knows you should never enter a cave alone. If he should fall and hit his head and drop into one of the sumps, he could easily drown. If he broke a leg, he would be trapped. And you cannot drink this water. It is so close to the surface you risk giardia, or worse. To be underground is risky business. To be alone underground is raising the inherent risk one foolhardy notch. As he prepares to climb into the dark, Spong reminds himself to be extra careful. Then he peers into the slightly angling downward crawl space with his headlamp and starts to pick his way headfirst down the narrow, boulder-strewn entryway.

The first twenty feet of the entryway descend at an almost 60-degree angle. In a couple of places, the Dubuque limestone formation opens up overhead, but the floor of the entryway is strewn with rock, and it is a careful climb down. He continues picking his way headfirst over the fallen rock. After the floor levels off, it opens into a larger crawling and sometimes stooping passage leading due east.

A few feet inside, the air temperature drops to 47 degrees. It feels cool and refreshing after his tromp through the weedy field and woods. And it is not as damp as Spong expected. His light wavers off the limestone walls. He settles near the bottom and gets his bearings, straightens his gear. He takes out one of

Ted Marshall, Rick Cunningham, and Ron Spong in Echo Lake passage, 1980.
Courtesy Ron Spong

his flashlights and switches it on. Now that he can stand, he can use the light to illuminate more of the cave passage. Then he sets off through the corridor and starts picking his way carefully through the dark.

One of the first things Spong notices as he stoop-walks through Hourglass Pass is the low water level. Normally the passage has a pretty good stream running through it, but today there are only low-lying pools of water with very little movement through the bed. It is the lowest water he has ever seen here. His pulse rises a little. When he steps into the Echo Lake Gallery, he is greeted not by a large underground lake but by pools, mostly small ones. In fact, even the Echo-1 Sump, wide and low as it is, is not as difficult and wet a crawl as it was during all their June visits.

Spong gets down low and pushes through Echo-1, getting only parts of his coveralls wet. He steps carefully across the thirty-foot passage toward the Echo-2 Sump with rising expectation. What he finds there both troubles and excites him.

Echo-2 Sump is narrower and higher than Echo-1. The narrow space means there is still plenty of water in the trap. Spong thinks there is just enough room to squeeze through Echo-2, but it will be a wet crawl. His coveralls will be soaked. He again wishes he had brought his wet suit.

What excites and at the same time worries him is the breath of wind. On their June excursions, they could feel the slightest breeze flowing into and beyond the impenetrable crevice they had dubbed Slaughter Canyon. Today the second sump is open and yields cool air. But instead of the air blowing in, it is rushing out of the narrow opening above the nearly flooded passageway. And it is too much for Spong to ignore. The opening beckons toward a passage that, to the best of his knowledge, no caver in the last two and a half decades has ever seen.

He bends down, steadies himself on some underwater rocks, and peers into the dark opening. He takes off his hard hat and shines his light across the top of the sump. It is not a straight crawl. And the ceiling rises a little. His very long legs sometimes get stuck, and he has had to dig to get around a tight underground space. If he gets stuck in the water, it won't take long before he becomes hypothermic. Hypothermia is a treacherous killer, gradually lowering a person's body temperature until muscle tremors give way to an absence of reason and finally unconsciousness and death.

Spong remembers both his obligations and the advice he has given to many other cavers over the years. He has had more than his share of close calls, in part because of what he is willing to do to open up wild caves. He wishes Ted or Rick were here with him, but he wonders if he will have another chance like this one. This sump has frustrated their previous attempts. And then he makes a decision.

Because he knows it is risky, he will take every conceivable precaution. But he has to try to see what lies beyond. They told him it was tall and—once you squeezed through some additional tight spots—it could be easily traversed, practically like walking down a city street. He bends down into the cold water, turns his head up, and lies on his side so he can prop himself up on one arm and keep his head above water through the tight crawl.

For a shocking moment the sudden cold takes his breath away. He tries to breathe in, tries to force an exhale. After several staccato hiccupping intakes, he is able to breathe again, and Spong starts crawling.

The first part of the sump is in a flooded, jagged crevice, which slowly ascends and widens with the air space gradually increasing. There is very little current. He pushes through about twenty feet of narrow, water-filled, rock-sharp passage. Finally he comes out the other side, soaking wet and cold. He climbs up into a higher passage. And after walking just a short way, what he finds stuns him.

Spong looks up and sees large speleothems—geologic cave formations. Stalactites hang from the ceiling of a side passage. Stalagmites dot its floor. He passes into a wide chamber; along its wall is a gargantuan flowstone. It looks eerie and otherworldly as he flashes his light across it. Over millenia, the mineral-laden flow of water has made a beautiful, organic-stained flow of stone. It is huge in the dark space of the cave, startlingly beautiful. Normally he would pause to take in its grandeur, its haunting, eerie beauty, but he thinks he hears something that reminds him he should not stay here long. Water flows somewhere ahead of him in the dark passage. There is moist air rushing toward him, possibly the harbinger of a back-flooding underground river. And that thought does more than worry him. The idea of a rising underground river is seriously frightening.

He pulls himself away from the speleothem-filled passage and continues working his way through the spacious cavern. He is soaked, his coveralls are wet, and the light breeze chills him. He starts to tremble, just a little. But what he finds ahead gives him a different kind of chill. Over two hundred feet down the passage, he comes upon a cross passage out of which water is running steady, deep and sure. This noisy stream has the look of a gusher, and it tells him to proceed with greater care. After another hundred feet, he encounters a second stream passage joining the one through which he now walks. Both streams combine and drop into a larger river passage. His flickering headlamp shines across the swirling currents, and he sees foam and debris, both signs of flooding. It tells him what he hoped he would not find. The underground river appears to be back flooding toward him. His pulse makes a sudden spike. The water may be rising. The water trap could snap shut.

He turns heel and hurries up the stream passage. He is pretty sure water is rising along the cave floor. He tries to focus. He must be careful of any misstep that could cause an injury. He barely notices the massive flowstone, the stalactites and stalagmites. He is wet and cold, but he can think about only one thing. He cannot get trapped here, where the cave wanders off into oblivion, where no other known entrance or exit exists, where he will likely work himself into a slow hypothermic state, with no water and no food and batteries running down. Katie and the kids are back at home.

He bends down and enters the Echo-2 Sump headfirst. It is the best way to enter tight spaces. He doesn't know if the sump rose while he was exploring, but he cannot take the chance. Everything is backward now. Finding the right purchase on the sidewalls and underwater rocks will be more difficult.

The passage widens, and he can turn around. He knows his long legs will have trouble wending their way blind through the narrowing, jagged tunnel. But there is no other way out.

Spong is cold, but this time the freezing water barely registers. He pushes and gropes with his feet, feeling his toes hit solid rock. He tries to remember his crawl through the sump.

His wet coveralls bunch up on the sump floor, and he has to inch back again to unsnag them. Several times he becomes stuck. Several times he backs up and pushes in a different direction to free himself.

The tight space overhead leaves barely enough room for his face, for his breath. He is soaked, and now he is feeling the cold. The gradual slope downward sometimes leaves his legs flailing for a purchase on the rock walls and sump floor.

Finally, he feels like he has reached some kind of open area where his long legs have a little more room to move. He pushes down into the opening, crawling through the last blowing-bubble space, and he feels himself get free of the sump.

Spong gives thanks into the shadowy darkness for his delivery into the Echo Lake Gallery. And he hustles down the entrance passage of the cave, cold and trembling and happy. He has seen some incredible cave. He has been foolhardy. He is not sure if he is going to share this discovery and close call with anyone quite yet, since it will require some explaining, given his penchant for safe caving. But it has been a remarkable day.

The old-timers were right: there is a lot of cave down there. Ron Spong thinks he has only scratched the surface. Providing the entrance stays open and the water remains low, he is looking forward to showing his friends those massive formations and exploring the length of cave that stretches farther into the subterranean wild.

10
The Unnamed Cave
Jessie's Grove and the unnamed cave
  (aka Coon Cave, Goliath's Cave)
Sunday, February 26, 1984

It is February in Minnesota, cold and dry. This far south, about five miles from the Iowa border, February is that month when the frozen world starts to turn. Though the days are growing longer and March is a mere three days distant, Jim Magnusson and his fellow cavers, Dave Madsen, Earl Clausen, and Harry Maiborn, are dressed for the cold. They have come down to this rural part of southeastern Minnesota to explore the twenty-five-acre parcel of woods known as Jessie's Grove.

Madsen gives a call out to the others walking through the trees.

"Found something," he reports, staring across a sinkhole to a small black opening in the limestone rock face.

"Doesn't look like much," Magnusson observes, "but could be."

"Worth checking out, anyway," Madsen suggests, and the others agree.

Madsen starts climbing into the rubble-filled hole, staring into the dark opening. "Looks like it slopes down into its own ceiling," he says. "Why don't you let me check it out first."

The others are more than willing to let Madsen have the first look, since it involves a tight, downward crawl. They all climb down into the wide, deep sinkhole, escaping the February wind as they watch Madsen carefully make his way head-first into the narrow, dark opening.

The explorers have come to these woods in search of wild cave. They are members of the Minnesota Speleological Survey (MSS), a nonprofit organization dedicated to the study, exploration, and conservation of caves, its membership open to all. Jim Magnusson, its current president, recently had some conversations with MSS members Dave Gerboth and Professor Calvin Alexander. Gerboth, who has belonged since 1980, has already logged almost two hundred caving trips, most of them in wild cave. He is the keeper of the MSS files, which have documents referencing two known wild caves in Jessie's Grove: Downwater Cave and Woodchuck Cave. Alexander has visited the region many times, in both professional and recreational capacities. His work studying the hydrology of Minnesota's karst region is well known, and he has made dye traces in Jessie's Grove and the surrounding area. Both Gerboth and Alexander have mentioned Jessie's Grove as a location for two known wild caves, and possibly others that haven't yet been discovered.

Magnusson is interested. In one of his first President's Letters, which introduce each issue of the group's newsletter, *Minnesota Speleology Monthly,* Magnusson articulates the Minnesota Speleological Survey's goal: "In my mind, a primary long term goal of the MSS is to discover, explore and survey every cave in the State of Minnesota." It is an ambitious goal but one the small MSS membership happily takes on.

In early February, Magnusson and classmate Mike Lilja were working on a lab for their historical geology course. Magnusson's eyes wandered over the map, and he was immediately struck by a place where the Dubuque and Galena geologic formations meet. In karst country, this kind of juncture sometimes results in caves. He made a mental note to enlist the help of some fellow cavers and do a little prospecting in the promising region.

Not long after Madsen disappears into the dark entrance, he calls back and tells his buddies to follow. After a pretty steep descent, the cave's entryway opens up, and after ten or fifteen feet the floor bottoms and levels out into a spacious stoop walk that disappears beyond the distant light of his carbide headlamp.

The four cavers are surprised by the length and openness of the passage. They keep walking down the corridor, and after more than a hundred feet they discover the first of three pools of icy water. It is 47 degrees in the cave, warm compared with a Minnesota February. But they can still see their breath clouding in the glow of their carbide headlamps. They cross two pools, and, finally, on the opposite side of a third long pool, the floor appears to rise and disappear into the ceiling. It looks like a dead end. But there is only one way to find out. Someone must make an icy plunge.

"I'll check it out," Madsen says. And he forges across the long pool, which thankfully turns out to be not quite waist deep. He makes an awkward, cold-jolting lurch through the dark water. At the other side, he bends down and peers into the crawl space. It looks open enough, and the cavers behind him watch the intrepid Madsen squeeze up the slope until his feet disappear.

After a short wait, Madsen's voice echoes back to them. "It's clear," he says.

Magnusson wonders how far it goes and whether it is worth the icy wade. Maiborn decides to have a look for himself, carefully crosses the long pool, and disappears up the slope.

"It's as big as Fifth Avenue!" Madsen's voice suddenly echoes. And it sounds like a big echo, produced in cavernous space.

Nearby Mystery Cave, the state's longest cave, privately owned and accessible to many recreational cavers, has a large section called Fifth Avenue, a wide, deep, long corridor big enough to accommodate a car. Nature took eons to carve the remarkably straight course out of rock.

Magnusson and Clausen look at each other and wonder if they are being fooled. A practical joke would be typical for the four friendly cavers. But Clausen is willing to take the bait. He steps into the icy water, crosses, and disappears up the black chute, while Magnusson waits and listens.

After more exclamations, Magnusson finally takes the plunge, and in a couple of minutes he is not disappointed. A huge, straight, east-west passage through the Dubuque layer of ancient limestone appears to stretch on into the darkness. Moreover, to the left of its entryway there is a gigantic, multiple-column flowstone formation as large and impressive as anything in Mystery Cave. Believing they are the first to have ever entered the cave, they name the spacious Dubuque passage Main Street. Clausen gazes up at the mammoth formation guarding its entryway.

"Let's call this guy Goliath," he suggests. The others agree. The name is a good one. Goliath. It sticks.

Over the next five minutes, they are startled by what they find. Opposite Goliath, a passage crosses Main Street and rises in a northeasterly direction. The corridor climbs fifty feet to the ceiling and is terraced with rimstone dams all the way to the top. Rimstone dams are created when calcite-rich water gets caught in shallow pools. The pools create stone-edged barriers or borders. Sometimes, as in this case, the pools terrace down the slow descent of cave and at the bottom end in a beautiful flowstone apron. Soda straws festoon the ceiling around a giant flow of stone high above. These long, narrow, cylindrical stretches of white stone the size of straws are produced by ages of drip-drip-dripping calcite-rich water.

The awed explorers strike out east along spacious Main Street. Where Goliath stands as a sentinel, the ceiling is over fifteen feet tall. The stone roof through the rest of the Dubuque passage continues tall, with heights over ten to

The Goliath flowstone formation near the entryway to the unnamed cave. Courtesy Art Palmer

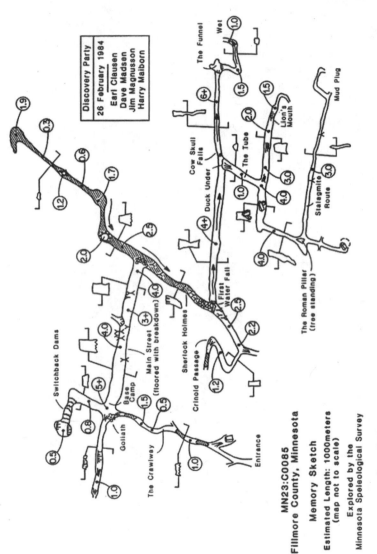

MN23:C0085
Fillmore County, Minnesota

Memory Sketch

Estimated Length: 1000 meters
(map not to scale)

Explored by the
Minnesota Speleological Survey

Discovery Party
26 February 1984
Earl Clausen
Dave Madsen
Jim Magnusson
Harry Maiborn

Switchback Dams

Goliath

Base Camp

Main Street
(floored with breakdown)

Sherlock Holmes

Crinoid Passage

The Crawlway

Entrance

First Water Fall

Duck Under

Cow Skull Falls

The Tube

Lion's Mouth

Stalagmite Route

Mud Plug

The Roman Pillar
(tree standing)

The Funnel

Wet

The map of the cave's introductory sections, made before it was named Goliath's. Numbers provide height in meters. Xs mark passages littered with breakdown, striated sections indicate underground streams, and cave cross-sections are marked with angled lines. Courtesy Jim Magnusson

twelve feet, for a length of over one hundred feet. The floor of the passage is periodically littered with breakdown, and the explorers have to step carefully over the ancient rubble. At the end of Main Street, they come to a narrower, smaller underground river. The river stretches from northeast to southwest. When they turn upstream, they find the river knee-deep or deeper, with the seven-foot ceiling starting to come down. Not far upstream, the ceiling descends to a crawl space of a little more than three feet. They turn around and move downstream, returning to a spacious passage with ceilings seven to ten feet tall.

They hear a waterfall up ahead and make their way toward it. Before reaching the falls, Magnusson sees another small stone curtain formation, and something about it looks familiar. Then it is obvious.

"Look at the shape of that curtain." he says. "It's Sherlock Holmes's exact profile!" And again, the name sticks. This passage will be known as Sherlock Holmes.

The short drop of water marks a point where another large east-west passage breaks off into darkness, apparently as large as Main Street. Downstream, the water continuance turns muddy, so the explorers backtrack to the new, relatively dry east-west passage. This channel is in the shape of a keyhole with ten- to fifteen-foot ceilings. They traverse the long passage approximately 150 feet, passing more cross channels cut into the rock. The east end of this tunnel drops into a tight crevice. It seems pushable, but behind them there appeared to be more spacious, easily traversed passages, so they retrace their steps to a promising southwesterly slanting corridor. Here they have to bend down to a three-foot-high, hands-and-knees crawl through the mud, but it opens up just the other

Ceiling channel in what is to become known as Baker Street, Goliath's Cave. Courtesy Art Palmer

side of the crawl, and amazingly they again encounter a spacious east-west walking passage with nine- to twelve-foot-high ceilings.

They push the east end of this passage, and, finally, for the first time all day, they come to a dead end where the cave walls narrow into solid stone. When they backtrack and head west, they find a sharp turn left into another spacious, southwesterly trending section of cave. Here the excited, weary explorers decide to take a break and sit down on a pile of breakdown blocks choking the intersection of the two passages. While they sit and rest, Madsen spots a ball of fur tucked into a nearby corner. It is a hibernating raccoon. They are surprised to find a raccoon this far back, but there is no telling its entry point. Careful not to disturb the animal's winter slumber, they move into the southwesterly trending passage to continue their exploration—but not before Madsen christens this intersection Coon Corner.

Just beyond the threshold of the new corridor, they encounter yet a *fourth* large east-west passage. Again, they are startled and amazed. The cavernous corridor is tall and spacious. As they head west, they discover beautiful formations, including one four-foot stalagmite they have to sidestep to pass. In a day of remarkable, incredible discovery, section after astonishing section, formation after phenomenal formation, the four men—perhaps the first ever to traverse this otherworldly landscape—decide to call this passage the Stalagmite Route.

The east end of this section is a tight belly crawl in mud. They have been in the cave for three hours. Finally, they decide to return to the Goliath formation, to the place that seems like the entryway to this extensive underworld wilderness. In the future, the Goliath formation at the entryway to Main Street will be their base camp. They now return to Base Camp to recover their survey gear and—because they have already been in the cave so long—begin the arduous task of mapping only a little of what they have found.

By 5:30, when they leave this remarkable underworld, they have surveyed only three hundred feet of the hundreds and more they estimate they have traversed. They are tired, wet, and cold. Shivering in the February wind, hustling back to their car, they are barely able to contain their excitement. This day, truly, they have done something extraordinary. This day they have probably been the first human beings to traverse a small part of southern Minnesota that can still be called frontier. Complete, utter, and unknown wilderness. And by their own reckoning and that of many others, they are indeed discoverers and explorers of a new, strange, and wonderful world.

The August 1984 *Minnesota Speleology Monthly* contains detailed accounts of the first three thorough penetrations of this cave, which has more than one name. Magnusson, who along with his companions still refers to it as "the unnamed cave," chronicles their underground explorations on March 4, March 18, and March 25. His "Cave Prospecting Update; March 4, 1984" begins,

> The week of February 27th was a very anxious week. Our curiosities were aroused by the possibilities presented by the stream passage at the east end of Main Street, so a few of us rented wetsuits to survey and push this area. Present were members Earl Clausen, Dave Madsen, Jim Magnusson, Harry Maiborn and Don Perrine. . . .

Since this time I have found out that fellow member Ron Spong had visited this cave after the sinkhole gave way, but that he didn't see the estimated 1000 meters which we have and that his progress was blocked by high water. Obviously the cave has dried up some, but I think we are talking about the same cave.

In the almost four years since Ron Spong entered what was then known as Coon Cave, he has not shared his detailed knowledge of the cave with many other cavers. And he has never discussed the cave with the MSS or any other caving organization.

Approximately seven miles north of Coon Cave, Ron Spong and his caving buddies have begun exploring, surveying, and studying the Forlorn River Cave System. According to Spong, this is an "extensive cave system comprised of several caves and springs that are hydro-geologically connected but not all physically connected yet."

Because of his earlier difficulty trying to penetrate the Goliath's Cave sumps, and because of his new discoveries at the Forlorn River Cave System, he has decided not to revisit Goliath's. He thought he had a pretty good idea of the caving opportunities at Jessie's Grove. During much of the year, Goliath's is simply too dangerous. He has been willing to focus on Forlorn.

MSS member Dave Gerboth learns about the 1980 investigations of the first part of Goliath's from one of the cavers who explored it with Spong (probably Ted Marshall or Rick Cunningham). When Magnusson finally shares his recent discoveries of what he thinks is virgin cave, Gerboth informs him about the earlier explorations. But it does not diminish the fact that Magnusson and his friends are the first people in a very long time (possibly the first ever) to have traversed all but a very small part of the new cave system.

When the five explorers return on March 4, 1984, it takes a little longer to reach Base Camp. They haul in wet suits, waders, lunch, cameras, and related equipment. It is tedious and exhausting work, and they finally get it all in to Base Camp by 10:45. First they walk around Goliath to explore the western passage behind the large formation, hoping they'll find even more open, spacious cave. Down a mud slope going west they discover a small room with a large flowstone formation that Perrine names Jabba the Hutt. To the right of the formation, they find another crawlway through the Dubuque limestone layer. The narrow space is beautifully adorned with more stalagmites and soda straws. They traverse it carefully to avoid disturbing any of the delicate formations, created over eons. They follow it for a little more than a hundred feet before it closes down to nothing.

While Perrine pushes a narrow crawl north off of Main Street, Madsen, Maiborn, and Magnusson don their wet suits. Clausen gets into his waders, and the four original explorers set off to investigate the watery northeast-to-southwest passage at the end of Main Street. First they push northeast, upstream along the river passage. After approximately fifty feet, they come into a large dome room with a jagged stalactite ceiling. The narrowing channel leads to another spacious standing-height dome room. And then it becomes very narrow farther on, requiring the three explorers with wet suits to crawl through the icy water with their chins and noses submerged. After another twenty-plus feet, they encounter another small dome room and another sixty feet of narrow passage beyond it. But finally, after 180 feet of pushing upstream, the passage ends in another sump, and the four disappointed explorers have to turn and start back downstream.

Perrine's crawl northward into the small passage takes him around 120 feet. Then it drops down through a narrow arched passage. He ends his traverse and returns with the others to Base Camp, where they finally pause in their explorations long enough to eat lunch.

Throughout the rest of the afternoon, they push more leads and make more explorations, but they do not find any more large passages that are easily traversable. They do add many more feet to their explorations. But much of it is, for one reason or another, a difficult crawl, climb, or squeeze. Magnusson concludes his entry with the following:

> Since we had already ate all the food we brought in, we packed our gear at Base Camp for the long haul out to enjoy the effects of a Minnesota March blizzard. We exited the cave just before 6:00 P.M. very surprised to find that the area had only received an inch of snow.

Magnusson and the original recent discoverers have been so struck by the cave's size, mazelike quality, and potential for vast new discoveries that they are spending every spare weekend exploring this new world. On Sunday, March 18, the four original explorers, along with novice cavers Dave Comer and Wayne Hromadko, drive down to make further explorations of the unnamed cave. Magnusson's entry describing this day begins with the following:

> We arrived at Mr. Kappers farm at 11:00 A.M., spoke with him about the cave and signed a release of liability. We were all assembled at Base Camp in Main Street by twelve noon. Tradi-

> tionally we have chosen to push when we first enter a cave since we are still quite fresh and enthusiastic. Deciding not to break tradition, we went to the west end of the falls passage to push the crevice lead to the right. (Northwest)

They push into the winding passage for over a hundred feet before it narrows into a watery passage. They find a crinoid fossil in the wall, which leads them to name this the Crinoid Passage. Then they turn around to pursue more promising leads.

They manage to push around the east-west Cow Skull Falls, and gradually the passage becomes a narrow crevice. They chimney along the crevice, their hands and feet pressing against both sidewalls up near the ceiling. More than ten feet below them they can see and hear the small stream cascade deeper below ground. They pass some more cross passages, though they are narrow. They continue chimneying east until they enter a stoop-walk passage that after another forty or so feet turns north into a watery crawl. None of them want to crawl through the stream, so they abandon this push, happy to have added another 150 feet or more to their cave discoveries.

Magnusson concludes,

> After reaching the truck I went back to check in with Mr. Kappers and to tell him about the day's discovery. He was delighted to hear the news and was anxious to have us complete our survey so he could get a better idea of where the cave went.

On the following Sunday, March 25, 1984, they again visit the unnamed cave to do more exploring. This time it is Jim Magnusson, Harry Maiborn, Paul Scobie, Bob Ehr, and Terri Sensmeier. In part, Magnusson's entry for this day begins as follows:

We all signed a release of liability and I brought it to Mr. Kappers and told him that we planned to take some photographs on this trip. As we walked to the cave Harry and I noticed the snow cover had diminished considerably from just the past week and Jesse's Kill was flowing a little higher than previously.

Finally, the same problem that plagued Ron Spong's earlier explorations halts Magnusson's. When they make it through the first part of the cave to the final sump, they find the water completely blocking the entryway up the other side to the Goliath formation, Base Camp, and Main Street. There is simply no way to enter the cave, and they must turn back. Moreover, through the rest of the spring and summer, they make several attempts to re-enter their underworld maze, but the last sump is always filled with water, and they are unable to push beyond it.

Magnusson's trip entries mention Tom Kappers, the owner of the property under which much of Goliath's Cave resides, and reflect his concern about potential liability. Tom Kappers, his wife Kathleen, their son Mark, and other members of his family are interested in seeing their cave explored and learning more about it. In fact, Jim Magnusson has kept Tom Kappers completely informed about all of their discoveries. He has also shared some of his photos of the place, including one of the massive flowstone formation they have come to call Goliath. Finally, Magnusson has told Mr. Kappers he needs to name his cave. Sometime between their last effort to enter the cave and the February 1985 issue of *Minnesota Speleology Monthly,* Tom Kappers decides on a name. In the newsletter's "President's Corner" column, Magnusson chronicles the eventful year of cave discovery and exploration in 1984, naming Goliath's Cave:

In February Dave Madsen, Earl Clausen, Harry Maiborn and I stumbled upon what is now known as Goliath's Cave. This gem of a cave was first visited by Ron Spong who called it Echo Lake Cave, but to Dave Madsen and I it will be forever known as the Unnamed Cave.

The same issue includes two more Magnusson trip entries: "Cave Prospecting Update; September 22 & 23, 1984" and "Cave Prospecting Update; September 30, 1984." About their September 23 exploration, Magnusson writes,

> We assumed the worst—the sump would be closed—and planned from there just to be sure. For this special purpose, Dave built an electrically operated pump capable of moving 10 gallons a minute, and smaller than a starter on an automobile. To power the pump we rented a portable generator, and also brought with us 400 feet of electrical cord and 150 feet of hose. . . . Mike Lilja, Dave Madsen and I left town late Saturday afternoon determined to see Goliath after waiting to do so for 6 months.

For the first time the cavers decide on trying to pump the water out of the distant sump. But surprisingly the sump has again grown shallower and now has four and a half feet of air space. They wade through icy water up to their waists. They are chilled but elated to once again easily enter the cave and visit their old friend Goliath. On this occasion and on the next Sunday, September 30, they continue exploring and surveying and taking photos of its delicate formations, enthralled by what they find.

The stage has been set for the cave's peculiar future.

Landowner Tom Kappers, who has finally given the cave a name that sticks, is aware of both the potential liability and the potential value of the cave. Not far away, Mystery Cave is privately owned and operated. For the time being, Goliath's Cave's potential value outweighs the Kappers family's concern over liability.

And Magnusson and other early explorers are frustrated that they can enter the cave only when the water is very low (usually during the winter). They begin to contemplate ways to make a permanent, year-round entry into the cave.

An hour's drive south is Cold Water Cave near Decorah, Iowa, the state's longest, most dramatic cave, declared a National Natural Landmark in 1987. Because the natural entry into that cave is through an underground spring (and usually requires scuba gear), the state leased rights from a landowner and, in 1972, drilled a ninety-three-foot, permanent shaft into the cave.

Magnusson now thinks digging an entry beyond the second sump would be an excellent solution to their Goliath's Cave entry problem. The pursuit of that year-round entry will seal the cave's fate for more than a decade.

11
Opening Goliath
Jessie's Grove, surrounding country, and Goliath's Cave
Sunday, October 7, 1984, through April 20, 1986

During the next few months, the explorations of Goliath's Cave add more than a mile of new cave to what has already been found. While no other gargantuan flowstone formations are discovered, there are similarly spectacular finds, including more waterfalls and sections of cave deep underground with ceilings that rise over two hundred feet into darkness. And the reputation of the cave, once a closely held secret, begins to spread throughout the local community and beyond. From its first probe by Ron Spong through the mid-1980s, the cave attracts a veritable who's who of Minnesota caving. And it attracts vandals. And perhaps more importantly, those who explore it are often frustrated by the same series of events that almost trapped Ron Spong that Sunday afternoon in 1980. That frustration—and dismay at the vandalism—lead to further surface exploration of the ground above Goliath's Cave and an effort to dig out another permanent entrance to the cave, one that can be locked.

On October 7, 1984, Jim Magnusson, Dave Madsen, Tore Dahle, and Mike Johannes enter Goliath's. By a little after 10:00 AM, they charge their carbide lamps and push beyond the last sump, stopping at the familiar Base Camp to have a bite to eat. After a brief repast beside the behemoth formation, they go on a tour of some of the more dramatic parts of the cave, including the Stalagmite Route. On the way, they discover a bottom crevice that looks large enough to enter. Magnusson goes in headfirst and finds a

> trickling underground stream flowing through a small tube-like passage with a perfectly flat roof. To the right (upstream) I could see for about 10 meters, at which point the passage appeared to Tee. To the left, (downstream) the passage turned around a bend. The passage is about 1 meter tall and the stream bed is about 1.3 meters wide. The floor and walls have many sharp scallops which made progress difficult and rather painful.

The passage is wet, too, and wends its way in a meandering course for several feet, to a point where Magnusson finally sees Madsen's flashlight shining on the opposite wall. Madsen and Magnusson spend more time pushing, but it is wet and cold, and finally they realize that if they really want to examine this drop-down passage, they will have to return with wet suits. They exit the cave by 2:30.

Over the rest of 1984, Magnusson and fellow cavers begin surveying the land above Goliath's, looking for promising sinkholes and other locations that might yield another entryway into the cave, something beyond the troubling forward sump that so often prevents their access.

On Sunday, February 17, 1985—a time they suspect the water level should be low enough so they can get into the cave— they decide to push the Drop Down passage in the Diversion Area off the Stalagmite Route. Not surprisingly, Jim Magnusson, Mike Lilja, and Dave Madsen are the intrepid cavers who plan the trip through the narrow passage where eons of flow have carved razor-sharp scallops in the walls.

They have told Tom Kappers they will be out of the cave and report back to him by 6:00 PM. By the time they haul their wet suits and related equipment in to Base Camp, an effort Magnusson finds more difficult than the last time, it is approximately noon. That gives them six hours of exploration, ample opportunity to peruse every section of cave they have already discovered and still be back at Kappers's farmhouse with time to burn. But Magnusson is already concerned about the time: "we really had no idea how much energy the day's anticipated discovery would require." With that in mind, they hustle out of their clothes and into their wet suits, consolidate the few supplies they'll need to bring with them, trim it all down to only the most essential survival and survey gear, and start off for the Drop Down.

They pass down Main Street, then take a right on the stream passage now called Baker Street, wade past the Sherlock Holmes section of Baker, and take a left at the unnamed passage, hiking toward Cow Skull Falls. Before Cow Skull, they take a right into the Tube, bend around Coon Corner, and enter the Stalagmite Route at the Roman Pillar. Now several hundred feet inside Goliath's, they finally take a left near the end of the Stalagmite Route and enter the Diversion Area. From here they have to crawl into the Drop Down. Madsen, followed by Magnusson and then Lilja, crawls to a place they have referred to as Rock Island. Up to this point, it is all rerun for Magnusson and Madsen. Rock Island, a narrow opening where they can get up out of the water and rest for a moment, marks their heretofore farthest point of exploration. They peer forward into more shadowy, water-filled passage. And then they keep going.

This part of the passage is narrow but at least tall enough to make traversing relatively easy. Uncharacteristically, the passage meanders along in a northerly direction for about fifteen feet. Here it is joined by a tributary from the west. They turn east (downstream) and soon find another cross passage that appears to lead into dry cave. But it is too narrow to enter, so they continue along the watery route, generally heading east but eventually turning north. The stream grows deeper, up to about ten inches, but it also becomes easier, because of the higher ceiling, to slog through the deeper water.

The passage continued meandering and remained absolutely unchanging—there were more scallops than ever and they were all razor sharp. We eventually reached a sharp turn left where the stream's depth was 10″. After making the turn we saw the day's first formations—stalactites all in a row and all cleanly cut at about the same length, with all suffering secondary fluvial deformation.

Here the passage also widens to over six feet, but the ceiling begins to get lower. Magnusson worries. To be caught this deep in completely unknown territory in a sump-prone cave is taking what little light and life you have into your own hands. If the water rises, the situation could be grim.

Madsen moves forward to check it out, while Lilja and Magnusson explore some nearby cross sections. Not long after Madsen disappears up the lowering route, his voice echoes back loud and clear.

"Come on up," he tells them.

The passage becomes progressively more frightening. Magnusson and Lilja wonder if the nerveless Madsen is leading them into perilous territory. In parts of this low, tight, dangerous crawl over a rubble streambed, there are only ten inches of air space above the frigid water. Magnusson will eventually name it the Character Builder. But after thirty feet, the passage quickly opens up to a series of stoops and crawls for over a hundred feet. They pass plenty of side passages as they continue to move forward.

"It would be nice if we came into a subway-sized walking passage," Madsen jokes.

Then suddenly they come to a bend in the stream, and the passage heightens to about ten feet with a wide triangular cross section. Here Magnusson checks his watch and notes it has been only forty minutes since they crossed into the Drop Down. He checks the time because all of them realize they have entered a major cave section that appears to run on into open darkness. They are fairly certain they are the first people ever to have walked here. They know their time is limited, and they want to keep pushing, so they hurry off into the cold, wet, open darkness, amazed by what they see.

Professor Calvin Alexander near the spot where Jim Magnusson, Dave Madsen, and Mike Lilja first encountered the new cave section. Courtesy Art Palmer

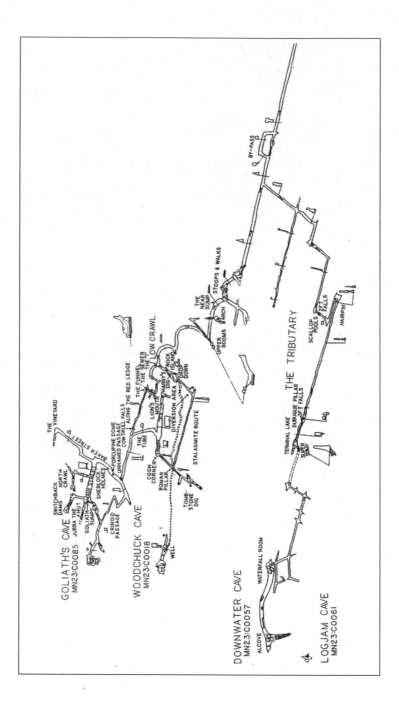

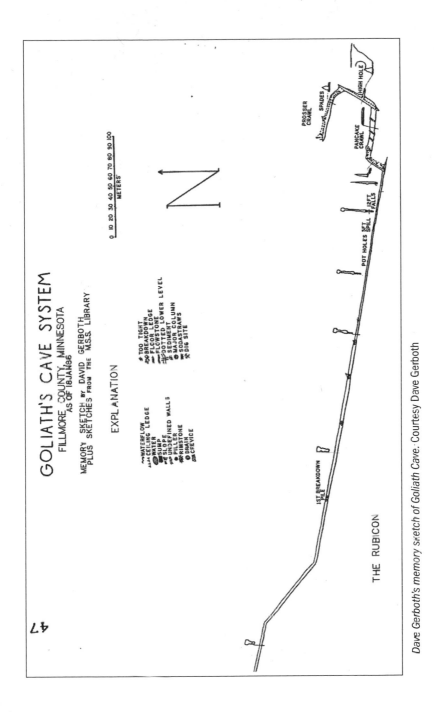

Dave Gerboth's memory sketch of Goliath Cave. Courtesy Dave Gerboth

Not far into this major passage, they find another large corridor coming in from the right, out of the south. This passage has a good stream flowing out of it, but they bypass it for now and continue moving ahead.

> A sharp left brought us to the day's heart-stopping piece de resistance. The passage again suddenly changed its cross section, this time becoming a 10 meter tall canyon, about 1½ meters wide at walking height from the streambed. The lower sections of the passage in the Stewartville retained its razor sharp scallops, but the ceiling was now observed to be the Dubuque Formation. The passage beckoned forward, straight as an arrow and ever taller. If we were surprised earlier, we were absolutely stunned now. Simultaneously, the 3 of us burst out in jubilation until our ears rang from the echo. We continued ahead.

They hike at a blistering pace down the straight, incredibly tall passage with the stream at the bottom. They climb over, under, or through large sections of breakdown, but their progress continues unabated for more than an hour. And they find debris along the way: a tree trunk, milk jugs, spray paint cans, and an old tire shredded almost beyond recognition. They guess the stream at high water probably forced the tire against the scallops and cut it to pieces. They don't want to think what it might be like in this cave with that much water. It would be an ugly demise.

Finally, the streambed begins to narrow, and Magnusson checks his watch. It has been two hours since they entered the stream channel from the Drop Down. He figures it will take at least three hours to get back to Base Camp and change out of their wet suits and then another half hour to haul their gear out of the cave, which would make it about 5:30 PM. That would give them a half-hour cushion, in case anything goes wrong or

A caver crawls under a portion of breakdown in the Rubicon passage of Goliath's Cave. Author's photo

they exit the cave more slowly than they entered it. More than anything, they want to continue, but now they are so deep into wild cave they know they must turn back. To continue pushing ahead, following the tall cave passage into the dramatic dark, would be taking more risk than is warranted.

Up until now, the discovery of new underworld passage has kept their adrenaline flowing at a fever pitch. But there have already been times when the cavers are feeling weary, tired, and overheated in their wet suits, which are now unzipped to their waists. Turning back, they begin to feel their tiredness. But they still have much ground to cover, and some of it is a dicey, cold, difficult crawl.

They make rapid progress, but it seems to take forever to get to the right turn. Not long after the turn, they cross the tributary corridor, and they cannot help themselves. They enter it and explore up into it for another fifteen minutes before turning around. They find more debris in this passage and assume somewhere upstream is perhaps a sinkhole or small opening wide enough to allow the trash to sink into and flow through their subterranean world.

After having found and traversed so much easy walking passage, none of the three explorers is looking forward to the forty-minute crawl and stoop-walk to get back beyond the Drop Down. But there is no other way to exit.

They take their weary bodies back into the tight spaces, back along the razor-sharp walls, back into the streambed with only ten inches of air space, crawling through the cold water, making their way through the meandering passage to Rock Island and then up out of the lower level and finally, finally, into the Stalagmite Route and back along the familiar passages until they reach Base Camp. They are exhausted. If they were not looking forward to making the crawl out of their new territory, they can barely imagine hauling their equipment down the familiar entryway to the surface and out to their truck. But again, there is no other way. They peel out of their wet suits, put on warm, dry clothes, and traverse over two hundred excruciating feet, crossing the near sumps and hiking down the streambed passage to the talus-filled entry and then out into the frigid day. By the time they get to the truck, they are fatigued beyond any recognition of weariness. But they are also elated. They know tomorrow they will be sore, tired, probably barely able to move. It will take at least a full day to recover. But what they have done on this day is again something extraordinary. They have been the first to traverse some of Minnesota's last frontier.

One week later, there is a February thaw. Magnusson, Clausen, Madsen, and Perrine suspect they won't be able to enter the cave. When they drive by the cornfield north of the woods, it looks like a rice paddy. They continue exploring the area. They finally enter an old driveway to an abandoned farm and park to eat lunch. Here they pull out a map and try to estimate how much new cave they explored in the past week. By knowing the direct route of the cave, their walking speed, and how far an average walker can traverse in two hours, they estimate they covered at least two miles of cave. Magnusson looks at the topographical map, estimates the location of the Drop Down area on the map, moves a little forward, and makes a 120-degree line across the map—roughly the same angle he guesses they hiked underground on the prior Sunday. They use this line to guide their exploration. They are looking for a large sinkhole, probably filled with trash. Area farmers have long known about these sinkholes and in the past frequently considered them natural dumping areas.

Finally, they come up over a rise and in the distance see a small patch of trees around a hole in a wide opening far off in the middle of a cornfield. They park the truck and hike over to investigate. And sure enough, it is big and meltwater is entering the bottom. There is much debris in the hole, including an old Model T Ford anchored at its base. With much effort they manage to remove the Model T, and beneath it there is a narrow entrance underground. But when Madsen gets down into it to push it, he finds it too dicey, wet, and muddy to safely probe. He snaps a few photos and retraces the narrow route, receiving an icy shower before rising to the surface.

But now the cavers believe they have found it—a possible new entrance to Goliath's. They suspect it will be too wet and muddy to dig for the next few weeks. But they'll be back.

Through the spring and summer, the only other natural entrance into Goliath's will be closed off by high water. They must find, or dig, another entryway into their underworld frontier.

When the weather becomes warm and dry enough, they return to the sinkhole and discover it ends in a narrow stone passage too small to permit the entry of the tire they found in what they now call the Rubicon passage. Discouraged, they continue searching the area for other promising sinkholes. They find some, but all turn out to be dead ends.

During the winter of 1985–86, Magnusson and other cavers continue explorations of the cave passage they have already discovered. They find that a tunnel of near cave called the Sewer provides an easier way to enter the cave sections that lead to the Rubicon. By chimneying along the Red Ledge to the Sewer, they can reach the downstream passages beyond.

Magnusson also reports the first evidence that someone has vandalized the cave. On Sunday, February 9, 1986, they enter Goliath's, turn south on Baker Street, and find someone's initials scratched into the rock wall. He references his discovery in one of his MSS trip reports, stating he is certain no MSS member would ever stoop to such desecrating behavior. But it means news of the cave has spread beyond the boundaries of the relatively small MSS membership.

During this time, Magnusson opens up the cave to other MSS members. He is still the point person and main contact for Tom Kappers, the landowner who must grant permission to those who want to enter the cave. Kappers always has them sign a release of liability and wants to know when they are going in and for how long.

On Saturday, January 18, 1986, Dave Gerboth, Larry Laine, and Steve Porter enter Goliath's to push the farthest sump at the end of the Side Tributary passage and to explore the Rubicon to its end. Both the Side Tributary and the walkable end of the Rubicon have already been explored. But there is a known, deep sump at the end of the Side Tributary no one has ever tried to enter. And beyond a waterfall at the end of the Rubicon, the ceiling drops to a narrow crawl space with scant breathing space. Porter wants to try to push it.

It is a full day of caving. The three cavers enter the Side Tributary passage and after several hundred feet it ends in a clear, deep sump, large enough to enter easily. From its edge, the clear pool stretches down into an angling tunnel and darkness. But without going in and trying to feel along the edges of the tunnel, there is no way to know if it opens up just

Cascade near the east end of the Rubicon passage, deep in Goliath's Cave.
Courtesy Art Palmer

the other side of a duck under or goes on into deeper under-water passage.

Gerboth watches as Laine and Porter both try to push the sump in snorkeling gear. Unfortunately, they discover the passage continues down into underwater cave. It is impassable without scuba gear.

They also hike to the end of the Rubicon passage, drop down the final falls, and push beyond it where the cave ceiling comes down to only inches above the stream's surface. Porter enters the stream and crawls over three hundred feet, with barely enough space above his mostly submerged head to catch a periodic breath.

This is Gerboth's 207th cave exploration. A compulsive chronicler of all his caving exploits, in typical breezy reportage Gerboth ticks off the seven major efforts of this long day.

1. We pushed and explored ceiling crevices along the Charac ter Builder.
2. We surveyed from the near sump to the start of the Side Trib-utary (the downstream portion of the Character Builder).
3. We went to the sump at the upstream end of the Side Trib-utary. Larry and Steve did some breath dives to determine if this was a duck-under. It was not.
4. Steve and I checked out a west side passage along the Side Tributary and I estimated we explored about 300 feet of cave.
5. We did a tape run of the Rubicon to determine its length. It measured to be 2,050 feet long. Also I did a compilation of the length from the Side Tributary to where the downstream crawl starts (this has not been surveyed yet). I estimated the length to be 2,330 feet long.
6. We crawled to the downstream limit and Steve went ~300 feet further to find seven inverted "V" joints and the aver-age airspace was 5 inches.
7. We exited the cave.

Around this time, Magnusson asks Dave Gerboth, who is known for his mapmaking abilities, if he will draw a good map of everything they have discovered to date. Gerboth creates a relative likeness of what they have found and explored.

In the May 1986 MSS newsletter, Magnusson reports that he and his crew of cavers have finally found the most likely place to dig a second entrance into Goliath's. With a second entrance, they surmise, they will be able to further control access to the cave.

> The ulterior motive in this decision is to have an entrance that is gateable. The landowner wholeheartedly agrees with my views in this matter for the above reasons and because it will keep any curious passers-by from possibly getting killed by a factor they would not be able to predict—namely the flooding of the cave. Although neither of them have been in the cave, both the landowner and his wife take great pride in their cave, and more especially its many beautiful formations. These picturesque wonders of creation as well as the cave itself will be quite secure once it is under lock and key.

The June 1986 issue of *Minnesota Speleology Monthly* has two accounts of further work at Goliath's. The first covers April 18–20, when Jim Magnusson, Greg Heideman, and Jeff Nelson decide to get serious about their dig. On a previous effort, they unexpectedly hit bedrock. So for this visit they bring down a jackhammer, three hundred feet of hose, and enough lumber to shore up three feet of shaft and to build an A-frame over the hole so they can rig up a rope and pulley system to more easily remove debris. They plan to borrow a compressor from Tom Kappers's uncle.

Unfortunately, the weekend is rainy. Finally, after the rain subsides, Magnusson uses the jackhammer to excavate two more feet through the bedrock. It is blistering work, and Magnusson and others are still surprised they have hit bedrock. They begin to wonder if they are digging in the right location.

The more they think about it, the more they realize they need to get underground and set up a survey station so they can make sure they are digging at a surface location that will lead directly into cave shaft. Unfortunately, the forward sump is already filled in, blocking any further entry into Goliath's. That means, given the time of year—spring and then summer and even possibly through fall, depending upon rainfall amounts—Goliath's will be closed to exploration. They could spend all three seasons sinking a twenty- to thirty-foot shaft that goes nowhere.

In the past, they have toyed with the idea of trying to pump the water out of the two forward sumps, at least to levels low enough to enable them to enter Goliath's. They have thought of using an electric pump, but it can't handle enough water to make it practical or useful for their purposes. Then Magnusson learns a gas-powered pump can discharge 252 gallons per minute. Some quick calculations have put the probable water volume of the near sump at around three thousand gallons. A gas-powered pump, if properly primed and set up, could empty the entire sump in fifteen minutes.

The obvious issue is the inherent danger of running a gas-powered pump in an enclosed space like this cave. Carbon monoxide is produced from the combustion, and if it becomes concentrated, anyone caught in the area would quickly become unconscious and probably die. And carbon monoxide, the cavers know, is insidious. It is odorless and colorless, and sometimes the first symptoms are light-headedness or a slight sense of inebriation, which can further impair judgment. For these and other reasons, the cavers have always decided against running a gas-powered pump on Goliath's sumps. But now they begin to reconsider.

12
Sinkholes, Sumps, and Gas-powered Pumps
The surface around Goliath's Cave, the sinkhole,
  and Goliath's entryway
May 2–3, 1986

It is an ambitious project and not without danger. But Jim
Magnusson, Greg Heideman, and Mike Lilja have planned
carefully. They will haul a 150-pound gas-powered pump over
175 feet into Goliath's Cave. Approximately forty feet before
the first sump, there is a narrow side passage where the cave

forks. Ron Spong's old map referred to it as Slaughter Canyon. It is too small to enter, but it has always provided an excellent source of airflow to the cave. Their plan is to set up the pump about twenty feet from the edge of the first sump. They will arrive Friday night, get the pump started and primed, make sure it is operating properly, and then exit the cave before any serious amount of carbon monoxide can build up and overtake them. The pump should empty the first sump in fifteen to twenty minutes. Eventually it will run out of gas and stop, and then the airflow from Slaughter Canyon will have the entire night to dissipate the fumes. Meanwhile, the three cavers will be camping nearby, up top. In the morning, they will enter the cave, move the equipment through the now mostly emptied first sump to the pesky second sump, and repeat the process. By Saturday afternoon, the second sump should be largely emptied, and the next twelve or more hours will clear the air. They will have Sunday morning to enter Goliath's and hike to the cave section they believe is directly beneath their surface dig. They can then set up a survey station and obtain proof positive they are digging in the right location.

There is risk, to be sure, and they are uneasy about it, but they believe they have allowed themselves enough room to make the venture viable.

Friday afternoon Magnusson and Lilja load his station wagon with all their camping and caving gear and related equipment and head south. Heideman follows in his car, hauling the gas-powered pump and requisite length of hose. By the time they reach the cave it is 8:30 PM, well after dark. They unpack in the cool night and make camp by lantern light, setting up their tent, rolling out their sleeping bags, and making sure everything is ready to turn in—once they finish setting up and starting the pump. They are excited to be in the early spring in the beautiful country of southern Minnesota, where the hills roll over Jessie's Grove and underground they know they will be readying Goliath's entryway for an unseasonably late passage.

Heideman drives his car as close to the cave entrance as possible, to minimize the distance they will have to carry the pump. The path is slightly rugged, and it isn't easy getting the engine down into the deep sinkhole entryway. Magnusson hauls the heavy length of hose down to the cave entrance. It is dark, and he sets up Lilja's Coleman lantern near the sinkhole entrance so they will have some light when they finally manage to exit.

At this point, Magnusson announces that he is tired and not up to getting wet and cold. He decides to cut some firewood and get the camp ready for Lilja and Heideman's return. It is 10:15 PM.

Heideman and Lilja spend the next forty-five minutes hauling the pump and hose approximately 175 feet into the cave. They stop and ready the engine and tubing. They affix the intake hose to the pump and run one end down into the water. The other end trails all the way out and up to the surface. Once everything is set up and ready, they start the pump.

In the deep confines of the cave, the engine fires, sputters briefly, and then enters into a steady, riotous drone. They take a moment to make sure the hose is primed. Thankfully, the Slaughter Canyon side passage, twenty feet behind them, is drawing a good breeze. They glance back toward it, ready to depart, and notice the output hose is kinked. They climb back and take a moment to set it right. It must make Lilja worry about their setup. He decides to crawl back to the sump and at least have a quick look to make sure there are no other kinks and it is operating properly. The engine has been running for only a few minutes. The air should be fine for a while.

Unfortunately, up ahead the sump has closed off the airflow, and the atmosphere in the small pocket, the start of Echo Canyon, is relatively stagnant. Lilja crawls up into it, turning a small corner and making his way down to the water's edge, where he presumably examines the hose and makes sure it is full and pumping water.

Back near the Slaughter Canyon entrance, Heideman waits for Lilja. When he doesn't immediately return, Heideman, too, crawls back to the sump edge. He looks around the corner to see Lilja squatting near the water's edge. Heideman crawls toward him while Lilja turns around and starts to crawl back to meet him.

By this time, the pump has been running a little more than ten minutes. They know they must exit the cave. The engine noise is roaring through the passage. Heideman idles the engine down and asks Lilja if everything is okay.

"The pump is working fine," Lilja answers. "But we gotta go. I have a headache."

Lilja starts to take another step. And then suddenly, unexpectedly —because all he has noticed is a headache—he falls to his knees. And he cannot right himself.

Heideman moves to the pump and hits the kill switch, and the engine dies. The cave returns to eerie quiet, but the sound of the motor is still ringing in their ears.

Heideman gets down to Lilja and shakes him. "We gotta get out of here!"

Lilja looks up at him, but his limbs are not working and he feels worse. Much worse. "I can't make it," he manages.

And then suddenly, without any warning, without even a mild headache or slight nausea, Heideman is overcome and almost passes out. He is dizzy but still coherent enough to know they *must* exit the cave. *Now.* To stay any longer is to risk unconsciousness. He makes one last effort to grab and pull the nearly unconscious Lilja, but Lilja is just too heavy and it is too difficult and in any case Heideman feels as though he himself is ready to pass out. He has no choice.

"I'm sorry, buddy, but I gotta leave ya," he gasps.

Somehow, over the next fifteen minutes, Heideman crawls the more than 150 feet to the cave entrance. He manages to climb up out of the deep-set sinkhole. Their camp is almost a football field away, and it requires all his strength just to reach it.

Magnusson is carrying a load of firewood when he sees Heideman stumble forward out of darkness. In as quick an outburst as he can manage, Heideman tells Magnusson about being overcome down below and that Lilja is still down there, passed out near the closest sump.

"When did you leave him?"

"11:15, I think."

Magnusson checks his watch. It is 11:30 PM. He can see that Heideman is unfit for anything but lying down and trying to recover his strength. But Magnusson knows they have to get Lilja out, sooner rather than later. "Let's go back and get him," Magnusson says.

"No," Heideman manages. "I'm so cold."

Magnusson realizes Heideman cannot re-enter the cave, doesn't have the strength to get back down under. And even if he did, he would be useless in hauling out Lilja's unconscious body.

When Heideman realizes Magnusson is thinking of going back down to check on Lilja, he pleads with him not to go into that enclosed space and endanger his own life. If he goes in now, he will likely be overcome before he can assist Lilja.

Magnusson knows he cannot bring the unconscious Lilja out alone. He has to turn to someone for help, and it better be damn soon. But it is after 11:30 on a Friday night. Tom Kappers is close, but neither he nor his wife nor any of the rest of their family has ever entered the cave. This is no time for them to learn the nuances of underground exploration, let alone rescue. He has to find someone who knows about caves, knows how to navigate them. He has to find another caver, and instantly he knows where to turn.

Just up the road, Steve Landsteiner is settling down for the night when there is an unexpected knock at his door. When he opens it, he is surprised to see his friend Jim Magnusson. They share a deep interest in caving. Landsteiner has been inside Goliath's and knows about Magnusson's ongoing efforts to open and explore it.

Magnusson tells him about the pump, about running it inside the cave, that Mike Lilja was overcome and is still down there. Landsteiner can see the concern on Magnusson's face, and he knows it is serious. Besides, the only reason anyone would come knocking at this hour is for help.

"Do you have any oxygen?" Landsteiner asks.

Magnusson tells him no, and they head out to Landsteiner's welding kit, unhook its oxygen tank, haul it out to Magnusson's station wagon and race back to Goliath's. They haul the tank out of the car and past the campsite. Heideman, still suffering from the effects of carbon monoxide poisoning, has crawled into his sleeping bag to get warm, to try to recover. He doesn't move as they pass. He appears to be sleeping, and they don't have time to check him. It is 11:58, approximately forty-five minutes since Heideman left Lilja back at the pump.

The tank is not easy to maneuver into the deep-set sinkhole. They leave it at the cave entrance and hurriedly enter the cave and cross the more than 150 feet to the pump and near sump. When Magnusson finally turns the corner to look down into darkness for the ailing Lilja, what he sees makes his stomach drop. An adrenaline rush kicks his heart rate up a notch. Lilja is lying facedown in the water. Magnusson rushes to him and lifts his head. Thankfully, he hears a shallow breath. But it is very shallow, and there is a gurgle sound to it—water in Lilja's lungs. And he is cold to the touch. Very cold, and soaked to the bone.

Magnusson checks his watch. It is 12:14 AM.

Landsteiner crawls down to help Magnusson lift Lilja out of the water and place him on his back on the dry cave floor.

"Stay with him," Landsteiner instructs. "I'll go get the oxygen." Then he turns and disappears into the cave's darkness.

Magnusson sits beside his friend. He gently squeezes Lilja's hand, searching for some response. But Lilja's cold, limp hand has only a faint pulse. Magnusson keeps holding his friend's hand, hoping for a miracle.

Landsteiner exits the cave at a record pace and heads back to the campsite. He will need help to hustle the oxygen tank down to Lilja and then get him out of that cave. He wakes the delirious Heideman and tries to roust him from his post-poisoning slumber. When Heideman finally comes fully awake and remembers their tragic evening, he looks up at Steve Landsteiner and after a long moment manages to ask the unthinkable. "Is he . . . dead?"

"No. He's still breathing. But I'm going to need your help getting the oxygen to him and getting him out of that cave."

The news brings Heideman more fully awake, and finally he gets out of his bag. They return to the cave entrance and muscle the tank down the steep entryway to the passage below. Then they start off as quickly as possible in a stoop walk down the corridor, hauling the oxygen tank down with them. Before they get to Magnusson, Landsteiner calls out in the dark.

"You okay?" he asks.

"Okay," Magnusson manages. "But I'm worried about Mike," his answer echoes back.

The air coming in from the side passage must have been sufficient to clear out the dangerous levels of carbon monoxide

Landsteiner and Heideman get the tank down to the prone Lilja. He is still cold to the touch, and though his breathing has become deeper and more evenly measured and he has begun speaking some intelligible words, he is by no means entirely coherent. The words Magnusson has heard are about Lilja being cold, wet, and near death.

Landsteiner sets up the oxygen tank and shows Magnusson how to administer it, holding it over Lilja's nose and mouth. Then Landsteiner and Heideman hurry back out of the cave to cut some tarp and poles and make some kind of stretcher, something they can use to haul the nearly unconscious Lilja up out of the cave. It will not be an easy exit.

Heideman and Landsteiner return with the gear and proceed to fashion a workable stretcher from the material. Lilja is still not returning Magnusson's hand squeeze. It is 12:50 AM.

By the time they get the stretcher set up, they tell Lilja they need his passive cooperation, and for the first time he seems to understand. They manage to place him on the makeshift litter, and then for the next almost sixty minutes they struggle with the prone, still largely unconscious Lilja. There is breakdown and water, and hauling an unconscious body, with arms and legs akimbo and the weight flailing every which way, is excruciatingly difficult. There is a steep rise to the surface at the end, and Magnusson worries about how they will ever be able to get Lilja up that rise. By the time they reach it, Lilja is coherent enough to understand what is happening. They ask him if he can move, and he lets them know he might be able to make it, and he gets off the stretcher and laboriously climbs the remaining few feet to the surface, using every last particle of energy to make it out of the cave entrance to the bottom of the sinkhole floor. But the effort exhausts him. He cannot move another inch. Lilja is freezing, almost incoherent, and totally spent. It is 1:45 AM.

They scurry out of the hole and retrieve Heideman's sleeping bag and come back down into the sinkhole and get Lilja out of his wet clothes and put him in the bag. There is no way the three of them, with the still ailing Heideman, can lift Lilja out of this deep sinkhole. They need more help.

Magnusson stays with Lilja, and Heideman and Landsteiner leave the cave site in search of more help. Landsteiner races to nearby Mark and Charlie Lichty's house. By the time they all return to the sinkhole, it is 2:25 AM. The four of them carefully carry the unconscious Lilja up out of the hole and into the back of Magnusson's station wagon. The nearest hospital is in Cresco, Iowa, a little over twenty miles distant. Landsteiner knows the way. The Lichtys return home and call ahead to let the emergency crew know Lilja is coming and what has happened to him.

The township gravel road gives way to blacktop, and Magnusson's station wagon races toward the hospital. They cross the border in record time and pull up to the emergency entrance. The medics, waiting with a wheelchair, wheel Lilja to the emergency room and start their examination. Lilja's body temperature is a startling, dangerous 81 degrees. He has a little water in his lungs, and the oxygen level in his blood is seriously depleted. The doctor begins treating Lilja's hypothermia, but the hospital doesn't have a respirator. There is nothing they can do about increasing the level of oxygen in his bloodstream. After an hour, his oxygen level remains alarmingly low, and finally the doctor calls Mayo One. In less than an hour, the emergency helicopter arrives. The onboard medics insert a breathing tube into Lilja's nose, and then they lift up, lift up fast into the predawn sky, speeding toward the Mayo Clinic, sixty miles away. It is 5:00 AM, a full six hours since the accident occurred.

Over the next two days, Mike Lilja makes a full recovery. The doctors believe falling into the sump and lowering his body temperature may have helped save his life. His hypothermic body lowered its respiration, so he took in much less of the dangerous carbon monoxide. He has no neurological damage. The prognosis is good.

Magnusson returns to their campsite, and he and Heideman get some badly needed rest. In the early afternoon, on their way to Rochester to visit the recuperating Lilja, they stop to tell the Kapperses about the accident. Magnusson concludes his accounting of the ordeal in the June 1986 MSS newsletter.

The sump had been our nemesis for about 2½ years now and we had thought about a gasoline pump before, but dismissed the idea. The airflow of the cave and the high rate of discharge of the pump got us to reconsider, but as it turned out, we should have stuck with our original intuition. We also learned what a monumental task a rescue can be, something which none of us had correctly conceived of.

The next day, other cavers who come down to work at the dig hear the harrowing story. Over the rest of the summer, work on the second entry intensifies. The Kapperses even allow Jim Magnusson and his caving friends to erect a small shack near the cave entrance. The building of what comes to be known as the Goliath Hilton, a one-room shack complete with carpet, insulation, a propane heater, a few bunks, and a small deck, occupies the cavers as much as the dig.

In September 1986, Dave Gerboth brings cavers Kent Parker and John Ackerman down to Goliath's to examine the cave and the dig. Ackerman, a dedicated caver and owner of Ackerman's Furniture Service, is thoroughly impressed with Magnusson's efforts.

Then, in December 1986, Magnusson and his colleagues are finally able to get into the cave with radio gear and confirm that their dig is directly over an open cave corridor. It is difficult to reach the underground location, but once there, they hear digging overhead, and subsequent radio signals confirm the position. They are that much closer to creating a second, man-made entrance to the cave, one that will remain open year-round. An entrance that can be gated and locked.

During the winter, Ackerman returns with Gerboth and is finally able to see Goliath's formations and front mazelike passages. He is struck by how similar some of the overall structure of passages is to nearby Mystery Cave—a cave in which he has spent much time exploring.

The difficult work progresses slowly over the next two years. There is much rubble and rock to dig and excavate from the pit. And as they work their way down to ten, fifteen, twenty feet, they have to shore up the sides with lumber. More pressing life concerns—and continued explorations—compete for time: the March 1987 issue of the MSS newsletter announces Jim Magnusson's marriage to Brazilian Julia Da Silva. Goliath's Cave becomes the second-longest cave in Minnesota, after nearby Mystery Cave. The June 1988 MSS newsletter recounts Jim and Julia's eleven-week stay in Brazil, where they visit Julia's relatives and explore some South American caves.

Eventually, the concern over potential liability begins to cool the Kapperses' enthusiasm for having cavers on and under their land. Kathleen Kappers learns that if someone enters the cave through an artificial entrance, the landowner's liability increases, raising it to an uncomfortable level. The cavers estimate they will break into Goliath's cave passage at around twenty-four or twenty-five feet. Finally they reach the twenty-one-foot mark, and they know they are close.

And then, with no explanation, the Kapperses call a halt to the dig.

On July 28, 1988, Tom Kappers posts a large KEEP OUT sign on the edge of Jessie's Grove. Next to the sign, lettered in red on a black background, is a posted handwritten note.

As of July 27, 1988 *Nobody* has Permission to be on this Property. *All* Prior arrangements are No longer honored.

The brief, initial, dramatic exploration of one of Minnesota's longest caves—and one that still holds much promise for new discovery—comes to an abrupt halt. At least for a while.

Almost one year later, John Ackerman cannot seem to shake Goliath's Cave's passages from his memory or his imagination. First he calls Tom Kappers and introduces himself and the idea he would be interested in buying the land containing the natural entrance to Goliath's Cave and the caving rights to explore it. Kappers listens to the idea but does not commit. Ackerman follows up his phone call with a brief letter, but Kappers never responds.

Ackerman is in Spring Valley most weekends because he is exploring a series of caverns approximately twenty miles northeast of Goliath's Cave. What he finds near Spring Valley intrigues him almost as much as Goliath's. When the Kapperses rebuff his offer of acquiring their cave, Ackerman negotiates with the owner of the land under which much of the Spring Valley caverns reside. By December 1989, he has purchased half the owner's farm, an acquisition that eventually leads to the creation of the Karst Preserve and Spring Valley Caverns, a cave farm of approximately five hundred acres with an additional 192 acres of underground rights. Over the next nine years, he and his fellow cavers blast, drill, and dig entrances to more sections of cave, until they have explored and surveyed 5.5 miles of new passages, making it the second-longest cave in the state. They also dig open and discover thirty-one additional caves on the property, all shorter than Spring Valley Caverns.

But Ackerman cannot forget his two brief explorations of Goliath's dramatic passages. And he has the maps and memories of his caving colleague Dave Gerboth to remind him.

13

Grinding Goliath into Gravel

Fillmore County Zoning Department
Wednesday, October 21, 1998

Norman Craig has been Fillmore County's planning and zoning administrator for over twenty years, and he can practically
recite the county's zoning ordinances by heart. He reviews
Thomas and Mark Kappers' application for a conditional use
permit and instantly knows what must be done.

After nine years of barring entrance to the cave, the Kapperses have decided to try making the blind valley known as Jessie's Grove economically viable. The parcel of woods and scrub brush located in the southwest quarter of the northwest quarter of Section 3, York Township, is heavy with solid rock and limestone. This corner of the Kapperses' property is filled with sinkholes, prone to flooding, too rocky and uneven to be tillable farmland. According to the conditional use permit, the Kapperses believe they have finally found a useful purpose for the land: they will turn it into a rock quarry.

It is an interesting idea. There are many other quarries in this part of the state. Only a couple of miles away sits the large Rifle Hill Quarry. In comparison, the Kapperses' quarry would be tiny, which raises a question: how much rock do they think they can extract from this site? And will it be enough so they can compete with nearby quarries like Rifle Hill? The limestone and crushed rock industry in Minnesota is a multimillion-dollar business, but starting up and running a quarry is a costly operation.

The conditional use permit does not address any potentially significant issues about starting a quarry there. But ferreting out the details, potential hazards, and public opinion about proposed land uses is what the zoning process is all about. In this case, considering the rural nature of that part of the county, Craig's office will issue notices to the Kapperses' ten nearest neighbors. There will be the usual public hearing over the site. Everyone owning property or living near the proposed rock quarry will have ample opportunity to consider the Kapperses' use of their land and to comment, both in writing and at the public hearing. At the end of the process, depending upon public comments and any collateral information (environmental impact statements and the like), the county commissioners will make an informed decision, voting to approve or deny the permit. Most permits are approved. Landowners have a lot of rights in the county, state, and country. If the Kapperses' idea has substance, it will be passed.

Craig's office mails the notice.

NOTICE

The Fillmore County Planning Commission will meet on Thursday, December 10, 1998, in the Fillmore County Courthouse at 7:35 p.m. to hold a Public Hearing on a petition by Tom and Mark Kappers acting as Kappers Limestone Products of Rt. 1 Box 70 Spring Valley MN 55975 to receive a Conditional Use Permit to establish and operate a new rock quarry on their property located in the sw ¼ of the nw ¼ of Section 3 York Township.

Norman L. Craig
Fillmore County Zoning Administrator

Almost immediately, the Kapperses' neighbors begin voicing concern and, in some cases, outright opposition to the quarry. Over the next two weeks, a widening chorus of opinions augments the neighbors' concerns. At the Fillmore County zoning office, the file on the Kapperses' intended use of their small corner of woods begins to swell. It seems there is almost no one who thinks the quarry is a good idea, from either a hydrologic or a geologic perspective.

The responses include one from Jeff Green, a hydrologist with Minnesota's Department of Natural Resources (DNR) who has done dye traces in streams that sink underground in Jessie's Grove and elsewhere in the region. He notes that a quarry in the area would have a significant impact on the pristine trout stream into which the groundwater from the proposed location of the quarry drains.

Eventually, the county commissioners turn to the DNR for a solution. Someone suggests the DNR could purchase the land and make it part of Forestville/Mystery Cave State Park, whose boundary is just a mile or less, from the site. Unfortunately, state law precludes the park from purchasing land outside its boundaries without an act of the legislature. While the legislature often expands the size of Minnesota's parks (as it did in 1988, adding Mystery Cave to Forestville), it is a time-consuming process, and no one knows if the state can act quickly enough to forestall the Kapperses' plans. At this point, the commissioners and other county officials are searching for a reasonable solution to their dilemma. Although no one but the Kapperses wants to see the quarry created, land ownership comes with powerful rights, and ultimately it is unclear what would happen if the Kapperses wanted to force the issue.

Several DNR personnel are involved, most of them out of the Rochester office or from the DNR's Southeast Region. By early December 1998, the controversy has landed on the desk of Larry Nelson, the regional administrator. He and Don Nelson (no relation), a regional environmental review specialist for the area, draft a two-and-a-half-page, single-spaced letter to Norman Craig.

Larry and Don carefully address each of the issues raised by hydrologist Jeff Green, Jim Wagner, area fisheries manager at Lanesboro, and other DNR professionals, without choosing sides in the controversy. For the time being, the DNR isn't sure what to do about the interesting location, with a blind valley and caves, including Goliath's, now listed as the third- or fourth-longest cave in the state (Ackerman's Spring Valley

Caverns has overtaken it) and which is known to have dramatic formations and passages. The Nelsons, and their professional staff, know that a quarry on the site would be a very bad idea. And that, ultimately, is the key point in their letter.

"We are not taking a position for or against the project at this time," they write, "but recommend the Fillmore County Planning Commission table a decision on this proposal until the information needs identified below can be satisfied. We are concerned about the potential for significant adverse impacts to stream flow and water quality in Canfield Creek, as well as local groundwater quality resulting from this project. A delay in decision will also give DNR time to explore land protection program options as an alternative to developing a quarry on the site." The letter outlines Jeff Green's dye tracing work, which shows the sinking stream makes a direct connection to Canfield Big Spring, the headwaters of Canfield Creek, the trout stream running through Forestville/Mystery Cave State Park. Further, the site contains caves, including Goliath's, that would be destroyed by the quarry operation. For these and related reasons, Larry Nelson suggests further research and information is needed to ascertain potential impacts to the area resulting from the quarry. He details four basic unanswered questions:

1. What is the proposed acreage, depth, and expected life of the quarry?
2. What is the nature and extent of the stone resource to be quarried?
3. Is there a mine operation plan?
4. Is there a quarry reclamation plan?

Under each of these questions, Nelson articulates some of the potential details involved and what will be needed to address those issues. Finally, Nelson concludes, "We are very interested in working with the landowners to identify land protection options that would compensate them to protect the area known as Jesse's Grove in its current state."

Not surprisingly, the public hearing on the conditional use permit, held the evening of December 10, 1998, is well attended. Six members of the county board are present, along with Tom, Kathleen, and Mark Kappers. Also present are twenty-three of the Kapperses' neighbors. After the usual motions to open the meeting and approve minutes from the last meeting, chairman Duane Bakke explains they have convened to field questions and comments regarding the Kapperses' proposed rock quarry, and he opens the floor for comments.

Neighbor Bill Hammersma comes forward and shares pictures of the cave system extending from under the applicant's proposed site toward Forestville/Mystery Cave State Park and the trout stream running through it. Hammersma is concerned that the blasting for the rock quarry would damage this cave system. Roger Sanford presents a map of the cave system, indicating the sinkhole on the property takes in water from six hundred surrounding acres or more. Venita Sikkink, who owns a farm of over three hundred acres directly across the road from the Kapperses' proposed site, expresses concern their rock quarry would interfere with her water supply, since she gets water from a spring that starts in the vicinity of the cave. The issue of dynamiting in the area is also discussed. Finally, the board members realize they need more information (and perhaps more time) to figure out a solution to their dilemma. A motion to visit the site is made and seconded, and the hearing is continued to the next meeting so the planning commission members can examine the site for themselves. After further discussion, the meeting is adjourned.

During this time, Professor Calvin Alexander has been fielding numerous inquiries from concerned citizens, reporters, and others about the proposed quarry. In response to an e-mail from one nearby landowner, Alexander writes, "Frankly, I would prefer to avoid getting involved in this controversy to the extent possible. Given the personalities involved, this issue could get very unpleasant fast." But he restates the Kapperses' rights as landowners and the hydrological issues about the site. He gives a thumbnail history of the opening and exploration of Goliath's Cave and mentions several geological reasons why he thinks the location is a poor site for a quarry.

The DNR's exploration of possible solutions brings them to the Scientific and Natural Area (SNA) program. This unit of the DNR, created by the legislature in 1969, is the kind of state government program progressive Minnesotans who love and use their outdoors are generally happy to support. The SNA's mission is to "Preserve and perpetuate the ecological diversity of Minnesota's natural heritage, including landforms, fossil remains, plant and animal communities, rare and endangered species, or other biotic features and geological formations, for scientific study and public edification as components of a healthy environment." As of January 1999, the SNA program administers more than 130 natural areas throughout the state.

Bob Djupstrom has been involved with the SNA program since the Minnesota legislature created it in 1969, and he has supervised it since 1982, presiding over its expansion from just fifteen areas in 1985. He is intrigued by the possibility of acquiring the Kapperses' forty-acre parcel and turning it into one of the state's scientific and natural areas. Because he is unfamiliar with caves and caving and does not feel qualified to judge Goliath's Cave's qualifications, he turns to several of his DNR colleagues who have extensive caving expertise, as well as to Calvin Alexander.

On January 28, 1999, he receives a detailed e-mail from Alexander in support of the DNR's efforts to acquire the location. Alexander references Jeff Green's work in the area and the existence of at least four cave entrances. He suggests the location is significant not only because of Goliath's Cave but because it is a blind valley. Nowhere in nearby Forestville/ Mystery Cave State Park or on any other DNR landholdings is there a good example of a blind valley. "Minnesota caves are a very finite resource," he writes. "Grinding it up into gravel and spreading it on local roads is a suboptimum use for Goliath Cave!" He concludes by noting the importance of preserving some of the speleothems that have been found in Goliath's: "The caver's accounts and pictures record a wealth of speleothem material in Goliath. Its acquisition could have major scientific significance."

Eventually, based on the geological significance of the site and the recommendation of the commissioner's advisory committee on SNAs, Bob Djupstrom agrees to add the forty-acre parcel, including the entrance to Goliath's Cave, to the protection list as a possible SNA. As he begins working with DNR officials and SNA advisors to acquire the land, Djupstrom enlists the assistance of Lee Markell, a DNR land acquisition expert.

Markell, an even-tempered, patient man, has worked on several land acquisitions in a variety of situations, some easy, some tense. He has a steady hand and a persistent nature. Over the next few months, he meets with the Kapperses on numerous occasions. The Kapperses begin to realize their conditional use permit is probably not going to be approved. There is too much public and local and state government opposition to the project. The *Spring Valley Tribune* carries an article about the controversy, including a photo of the impressive formation for which the cave is named, with Madsen, one of the cave's earliest explorers, standing beside it.

Unbeknownst to Calvin Alexander and others not directly involved in the negotiations for the Kapperses' land, in April 1999 the DNR signs an option to purchase the property. Since there is little likelihood the acquisition will not occur, the SNA lists the site in a new version of *A Guide to Minnesota's Scientific and Natural Areas*, published the same month. Each SNA entry includes directions on how to get to the location, a simple map, a site description, and related information. The directory's listing for "Goliath Cave" carries this cautionary warning:

> Note: To ensure public safety, entry to the gated cave system is subject to written permission. Researchers and qualified spelunkers should apply through the Minnesota DNR; SNA Program (651) 296-2835. Visitors may explore the land above the cave at any time without permission, however.

For a while the publication of the Goliath's Cave entry goes unnoticed by regional cavers. But when the listing comes to the attention of the MSS, it sends a shock wave through the caving community. In a phone call and subsequent letter to DNR Commissioner Allen Garber, Calvin Alexander expresses his concerns: "This is the first time that the biologically oriented SNA program has acquired a SNA containing a cave and I am very concerned that the SNA staff do not understand or appreciate the difficulties of managing such a resource without destroying it. . . . The field of cave management is well developed. Annual Cave Management Conferences have been held for a number of years and Proceedings of those Conferences are available." Cave management professionals agree that publicizing cave locations without any management in place is "an open invitation for their destruction through vandalism of the caves, their formations and any biology therein." The web page and SNA directory entries could mean the speleothems the SNA wants to save "MAY NOT BE THERE by the time the DNR acquires and gates the cave(s)."

Alexander's letter describes Goliath's Cave as a death trap to the uninformed caver. He still believes "that state ownership of this property is the best possible way to protect the resource and the public." But he is worried "Goliath Cave may not survive the SNA staff's learning curve." In addition, he recommends they find some other name for the area.

Indeed, the notice of Goliath's Cave as the newest SNA property on both its web site and in the pages of the SNA directory also prompts some non-DNR cavers to visit the site. Suddenly, some cavers believe the cave is no longer owned by the Kapperses.

On a late afternoon that November, Jim Magnusson, Greg Heideman, and several others gather again to enter and explore the cave. The caving trip is to be a kind of farewell for Magnusson, who for a half-dozen years led the discovery, exploration, inventorying, mapping, and naming of many of Goliath's Cave's features. He is moving to Brazil, where he has taken a job to join his wife and young daughter. Present are almost a dozen cavers. Some, like Heideman and Jeff Nelson, have already been in Goliath's, and others are first-time cavers. Magnusson and Heideman are not current members of the MSS. No one in the MSS was notified of the trip.

Magnusson and his fellow cavers are probably happy to think the Kapperses no longer own the property. But if they know about the SNA's acquisition, or pending acquisition, they apparently don't know, or ignore, the SNA's application process.

When the cavers exit the cave, two men are waiting for them. One is Tom Kappers and the other, a man in his twenties, appears to be Mark Kappers. Heideman, at the head of the group, speaks with the landowners. The younger man informs them they are trespassing, that the cave and the land on which they are walking is still owned by the Kapperses, and they will be reported to the county sheriff and prosecuted for trespassing. After several words are exchanged, the cavers pile into their three vehicles and drive away.

The Kapperses, who have recorded their license plate numbers, inform the authorities of the trespass, but no charges are filed.

Unfortunately, the trespass and illegal entry into a wild cave is widely discussed in Fillmore County and throughout the DNR and the MSS's small caving community. While no one is ever charged, and none of the cavers in Magnusson's group were active MSS members, the reputation of the club is badly tarnished by the incursion. The incident convinces Bob Djupstrom and others within the DNR that the sooner the cave is gated, the better. They also recognize that as soon as the SNA finalizes the acquisition, they will have to put in place strict measures to make sure the cave (and the public) is protected.

Sometime in 1999, John Ackerman, who first tried to buy the natural entrance to Goliath's Cave in 1989, has heard that the Kapperses might be interested in selling their land. Ackerman's Furniture Service has continued to do well in recent years, providing the monomaniacal caver with additional resources to acquire southern Minnesota land in order to open, explore, survey, inventory, protect, and conserve more Minnesota caves. Since his December 1989 acquisition of Spring Valley Caverns, he has also purchased a large customized trackhoe power shovel he has dubbed the Cave Finder. He uses the Cave Finder to make rapid work of digging out sinkholes and other promising cave leads. With the Cave Finder, Ackerman can accomplish in one day what might take weeks or longer for manual diggers to achieve.

On a warm afternoon in the fall of 1999, John Ackerman gives the Kapperses another call, on the outside chance they might be willing to consider selling him the forty-acre parcel. His phone call is answered by Kathleen Kappers.

When he reiterates his proposal to her, she mentions the land is religious to her.

John Ackerman doesn't understand. "If it's religious, why would you desecrate it by placing a quarry on it?"

The line goes dead.

Jeff Green, the DNR hydrologist, tells the SNA to be sure they acquire *all underground caving rights* to the site. Much of Goliath's Cave extends beyond the Kapperses' property. If John Ackerman or other parties were to acquire underground rights to the rest of the cave and find or dig an entrance into it, they would be able to access this underground wilderness of waterfalls and geologic formations. The effort to acquire all of the cave's underground rights would require negotiations with and payments to other neighbors, but it is the only way to ensure that all of Goliath's Cave will remain protected in the SNA's hands.

Others in the DNR and SNA agree with Green's assessment. They begin talking with the owner of the eighty acres directly north of the site. Mark White, supervisor of Forestville/Mystery Cave Park, also recommends the DNR acquire either the land or caving rights to the land that lies directly east of the new SNA site. Venita Sikkink's farm sits over a very large part, perhaps the majority, of Goliath's Cave.

Unfortunately, there is currently no money for additional DNR acquisitions, and the state will have to wait before attempting to buy more property in the area.

On November 16, 1999, Commissioner Garber answers Professor Alexander's October 20 letter on the SNA's acquisition and management of Goliath's Cave. Agreeing that the SNA directory listing and web page were premature, he points out that acquisition of the property will soon be finalized. But Garber disagrees with Alexander's reference to the "lack of consultation with other DNR personnel knowledgeable about cave management." In May, Garber explains, just such people were consulted. They suggested the creation of a management committee of informed professionals to advise the SNA on how best to oversee the resource. When DNR professionals visited the site, with the landowner's permission, they "discussed gating strategies, as well as the structure of a management team.

These visits did not, for instance, reveal any damage within the cave nor was recent visitation by others evident. Based on these visits, the DNR anticipates having the cave gated in about a month."

And finally, he invites Professor Alexander to be part of the management committee: "In this respect I would like to offer you the opportunity to sit on this team so as to provide your expertise and knowledge in assisting the Department in developing the management recommendations for this special resource."

As a result of these exchanges, Bob Djupstrom confers with Mark White, Warren Netherton, the DNR's cave naturalist in charge of Mystery Cave, and others over the choice of a new name for the Goliath's Cave SNA. In the April 2000 directory, it is rechristened Cherry Grove Blind Valley SNA.

And Alexander accepts Djupstrom's offer to be on the site's management committee. The committee will be somewhat informal, and Calvin Alexander will be the only non-DNR member.

Finally, Lee Markell gets an appraisal of the land. Recognizing the depth of opposition to the quarry and seeing a fair offer, the Kapperses finalize the sale. On January 21, 2000, the state of Minnesota pays $89,100 for the parcel of land containing numerous sinkholes, a blind valley, trees, brush, and the entrance to a few caves, including Goliath's. The SNA adds the first cave to its growing list of Scientific and Natural Areas. But before any member of the public has a chance to enter it, the entrance is promptly closed with a steel gate and locked. Anyone seeking entrance into the cave must apply using a permitting system administered by the DNR. No exceptions.

The gate, and the DNR's permitting system, are immediately controversial. Dave Gerboth, Neal Hines, Calvin Alexander, John Ackerman, and just about everyone else in the MSS membership consider the policy an insult.

But the DNR is not swayed by the amateur cavers' arguments. Moreover, to ensure there is no doubt as to their intention, and to avoid any other potentially harmful and unwanted incursions into the cave, the DNR commissioner's order dedicating the site as an SNA sets forth the management regulations for visitation and use of the site. The order is made public, and portions of the rules are placed on a sign that is erected on the Cherry Grove Blind Valley SNA boundary.

> It shall be illegal for any person to possess on their person any caving equipment, shovel, pry bar, hammer, torch or other tool

The locked steel gate across the natural entrance to Goliath's Cave, about 2006. Author's photo

or instrument that could be used to damage or move gates, fences, stone, soil or the subsurface or gain entry below ground while on the site without a written permit from the Commissioner of Natural Resources.

The perspectives about the best way to manage the site are already beginning to calcify around two viewpoints having everything to do with access. On one side is the DNR. On the other is most of the MSS membership. Both sides believe they represent the best interests of the public. And both sides are certain their perspectives are right and should prevail. No one can predict how these different perspectives will play out.

14
The Meeting
Room 110, Pillsbury Hall, University of Minnesota, Minneapolis
July 11, 2001, 7:00 pm

The 81-degree high for the day has moderated to 75, but the evening air still feels muggy. The huge yellow and red sandstone blocks of the University of Minnesota's Pillsbury Hall, built in 1887, are a memorable fixture on campus and a fitting edifice for the Department of Geology and Geophysics. But the stone has done little to lower the spacious old lecture hall's temperature. Inside, Calvin Alexander crosses the hallway from his office and greets the evening's guest speaker, Bob Djupstrom, the Scientific and Natural Area program's supervisor.

Alexander's hair is snow white, and the six-foot-one professor's vigorous, sturdy frame attests to a life spent exploring the world's wilder regions, aboveground and below. His metal-rimmed glasses sparkle in the overhead florescent glare. His eyes are at the same time sober and humorous, like the rest of his demeanor.

Professor Alexander is one of those rare individuals who has made a living doing what he loves—exploring the world's geology and teaching like-minded youth about the captivating world of rocks and water. He is a specialist in hydrogeology, the distribution and movement of water through the soil and rocks of the earth's crust. He is a member of several professional organizations and societies committed to the study of hydrology, geology, or geophysics. In 1997, he won the Horace T. Morse–Minnesota Alumni Association Award for Outstanding Contributions to Undergraduate Education. And he has published numerous articles in professional journals and books. He has also been a frequent consultant on several different types of projects having to do with hydrology, hydrogeology, and karst regions.

But perhaps most important of all, at least as it concerns tonight's presentation, Calvin Alexander knows Minnesota's southeastern regions. He knows the landowners. He knows the caves. He knows the geology and hydrology of the region. And he straddles the academic, governmental, and public caving worlds. Which is why, this night, he is glad Bob Djupstrom has come to speak to the fifteen or so assembled members of the Minnesota Speleological Survey.

Like other cavers in the MSS, Alexander had long known about Goliath's Cave, which he recognizes as one of the state's better examples of a karst blind valley and cave. He appreciates the fact the DNR/SNA saved the cave, and he toured it for the first time as a member of the SNA management committee, shortly after the acquisition.

But he has been frustrated by the subsequent management of the site. First, the SNA staff stumbled in announcing their ownership before the land was actually acquired. Second, they immediately gated the cave, refusing entry to qualified members of the public. And finally, there is the management committee's schedule: it has convened just three times.

Their first meeting, on December 9, 1999, was highly successful. Not only did they get to tour the cave, but their initial conversations about how best to map, inventory, and manage this resource were convivial, useful, and informed. The members, all of whom attended the meeting, included Don Nelson, DNR regional environmental review specialist; Ellen Fuge, DNR/SNA management specialist; Jim Wagner, DNR area fisheries supervisor; Mark White, Forestville/Mystery Cave State Park supervisor; Warren Netherton, DNR cave specialist; Jeff Green, DNR regional groundwater specialist; Gerda Nordquist, DNR county biological survey; and Calvin Alexander. Nordquist and Alexander are both MSS members.

During their second meeting, on December 21, 1999, they received an update on the acquisition, which would be finalized in a month. They also reviewed the commissioner's designation order and discussed site inventory and research, criteria for entering the cave, and overall site management.

On May 4, 2000, they met and continued mulling management concerns. Alexander suggested the management of the cave be opened up to include other non-DNR representatives. He also made proposals for surveying and inventorying the cave. Before Mystery Cave became part of the Minnesota park system, Alexander, working with the MSS and other recreational cavers, made the first survey and map of its numerous mazelike passages.

During those last two meetings, the professor sometimes felt like the outsider he was, that his views were sometimes dismissed or ignored, albeit politely. Ultimately, his suggestion that other public, non-DNR members be given a voice in how the cave would be managed was rejected, as was his suggestion that the SNA move forward with a surveying effort, an effort with which he knew MSS members could ably assist.

Not long after the cave was gated, Djupstrom, with the concurrence of most members of the committee, decided the cave would not be opened to anyone except by permit. Originally, the SNA guidebook indicated that "Researchers and qualified spelunkers should apply" if they wanted to enter the cave. But on further analysis, it made more sense to Djupstrom and others in the DNR that the cave be closed for its own protection, except to scientific research that could be granted through the SNA's permitting process. Before any more surveying work would be done, the DNR needed to develop cave mapping protocols.

Alexander and the other MSS members, using measurements of length and compass headings as well as direct memory, had already drawn and published two detailed maps of the cave. The DNR/SNA had also used a large photo book detailing some of the cave's more dramatic features that Jim Magnusson had produced with contributions from MSS members. The Kapperses loaned the book to the DNR/SNA, who had used it while deciding whether or not to purchase the land. To some in the MSS, it seemed as though the mapping and inventory work already accomplished by the MSS—proof of its capabilities and expertise, now to some extent being relied upon—was being ignored.

Tonight, Calvin Alexander and Bob Djupstrom are joined by Dave Gerboth, the maker of one of those maps, who has poked into more corners of the huge cave system than almost anyone else present. He has made literally hundreds of explorations into Minnesota's wild caves in the last thirty years. Gerboth, like others in the room, considers himself a careful conservationist. And like others, he was surprised and then unhappy with the SNA's unwillingness to let club members enter the cave.

Several other MSS members are here, including Neal Hines, the MSS newsletter editor, and Daniel Doctor, one of Alexander's doctoral students, who is writing a dissertation on the hydrogeology of the classical karst of Slovenia.

Doctor, who has been out of the country for the last twenty-seven months gathering data for his dissertation, has not been part of the controversy surrounding the state's ownership of Goliath's Cave. Doctor is both a knowledgeable geologist and an ardent caver. He recognizes the informed, contributing role members of local caving communities can provide to public governmental organizations like the DNR/SNA and to academia. He is also profoundly familiar with the fragility of cave environments and with the potential danger of caves. Like his dissertation supervisor, Daniel Doctor is a geologic diplomat, artfully straddling the worlds of academia, science, government, and recreational caving.

Bob Djupstrom is a slim, athletic five feet eight inches. He has intent, coffee-colored eyes and dark brown hair. As the supervisor of the SNA, Djupstrom recognizes he represents both the DNR and his own program. For public meetings like this one, at which he is the scheduled speaker, he is careful to wear appropriate attire. The MSS meetings are informal, so tonight he wears light brown cotton slacks and a comfortable short-sleeved shirt. And now he rises at the front of the room, confident and at ease in front of the small gathering.

Djupstrom's certain command of the SNA's facts and objectives conveys both his sincerity about the program and his conviction about its mission. He recognizes his role is as steward of these scientific and natural areas, now numbering 135: he won't be working forever. The DNR's SNA program and the preservation of those parcels for scientific and educational purposes—for generations to come—is really all that matters. And frankly, he is a little surprised about what he has heard regarding some of the MSS membership and their perspective about the SNA's management of Goliath's Cave. Djupstrom believes the MSS should be happy the SNA saved the cave from certain destruction. Without the SNA's acquisition of the site, no one would be in this room tonight. The cave might already have been ground up and spread on rural county roads.

Djupstrom begins his presentation by telling the assemblage about the SNA program and some of the sites it manages, including the Cherry Grove Blind Valley location. He speaks with measured pride, reiterating the SNA's primary mission: "to restore Minnesota natural habitat that has statewide significance to its 1850 state." The SNAs do not have hiking trails or camping facilities or privies; the DNR administers state parks, trails, forests, and other areas for that kind of public use.

The SNA program is assisted in its oversight, he explains, by a Commissioner's Advisory Committee, consisting of members in academia and other qualified people. The advisory committee helps the SNA make policy decisions regarding the SNA sites. Then Djupstrom gives some background on the Cherry Grove Blind Valley acquisition. He tells the MSS how the DNR first came to know about the property, then recognized the threat of development, and ultimately stepped forward and rescued the site by acquiring it.

Members nod in appreciation. Everyone in the room is, in fact, more than a little thankful for the SNA's acquisition of the land, and those who have been in the cave know better than anyone what has been saved.

Djupstrom explains that because he has little familiarity with Minnesota's caves, he assembled an informal management committee of experts who can make recommendations on the site's management. Djupstrom names the team's current members, identifying those who are MSS members, and describes their qualifications.

On their advice, and that of DNR professionals, Djupstrom and the SNA have decided the best course of action is to strictly control access into the cave, a decision the management committee supported.

Djupstrom also tells the MSS members their organization may be asked, in the future, to assist with completing a survey and inventory of the cave. But that would only occur under a DNR plan using specific protocols, yet to be developed, to ensure the cave and its system is surveyed, inventoried, and managed using the best scientific and professional means available. He acknowledges the already extensive surveying, inventorying, and photographing of the cave that has largely been completed by the MSS and its membership and expresses his appreciation.

There must be no ambiguity, though, over the gating and controlled access to Goliath's Cave. The SNA's sign quotes pertinent parts of the DNR commissioner's order. Djupstrom wants to impress upon the recreational cavers that no entry similar to the illegal entry that occurred in the fall of 1999 will be tolerated.

More to the point, he quotes from Minnesota Statute 86A.05, Subdivision 5, which describes the purpose of the program, how the units are to be administered, the qualifications of its units, and how they are to be designated: "(a) A state scientific and natural area shall be established to protect and perpetuate in an undisturbed natural state those natural features which possess exceptional scientific or educational value." Units must have "natural features of exceptional scientific and educational value"; one criterion specifically covers "natural formations or features which significantly illustrate geological processes." Goliath's Cave was added to the system precisely because it passed the difficult test for SNA authorization. Further, he explains, the SNA is required to give these areas one of three designations, depending upon the area's qualifications: a *research unit*, an *educational unit*, or a *public use unit*. The dangers posed by the sump clearly make the Cherry Grove Blind Valley SNA unfit for designation as an educational unit, which allows access by primary, secondary, and college undergraduate programs, or as a public use unit. This SNA has been designated a research unit, and language governing its administration clearly states, "Use is limited to programs conducted by qualified scientists and college graduate and postgraduate students."

Djupstrom concludes by describing the SNA's desire to acquire the eighty acres directly north of the sinkhole entrance to Goliath's Cave. Whenever there are heavy rains, runoff from the property, which is under cultivation, flows into the sinkhole, carrying with it surface soil and other debris that clog and dirty the cave. Restoring the land to natural prairie would diminish the surface runoff. Everyone agrees it is an excellent idea.

Finally comes the moment for which most of the assembled MSS membership has been waiting: the question-and-answer period.

Daniel Doctor, Calvin Alexander, Dave Gerboth, Neal Hines, and other MSS members prevail on Djupstrom to understand the cavers' perspectives. In a terse back-and-forth, they take a few minutes to emphasize for Djupstrom certain aspects of the club's purpose and membership.

The organization, "dedicated to the study, exploration and conservation of caves," has already discovered, opened, surveyed, inventoried, and documented more miles of cave than any other organization in the state. Its few members *are* the experts. And they come from all walks of life—"cave explorers, conservationists, cave owners, cave scientists, students, and anybody who is interested in caves," including academics like Alexander and regular working citizens like Gerboth. They share a common perspective and goal. The MSS membership has a deep fascination with the underground world, a pro-found respect for its dangers, and a total commitment to main-taining the pristine quality of environments in which few men and women have trod.

Djupstrom reaffirms that no recreational caving of any kind will take place in the cave for the foreseeable future, un-der any circumstance.

The irritation in the room ratchets up a notch.

Djupstrom reiterates that until logical, comprehensive sur-veying protocols are in place, it would be counterproductive to enter and map the cave. Warren Netherton, the DNR's cave specialist, is currently drafting those cave mapping protocols for work in Mystery Cave. When they are finished, those same protocols will be used to map and inventory Goliath's Cave.

The clash of perspectives may be inevitable. Djupstrom con-veys the SNA's commitment to his program's legislative man-date and to best professional standards with utter conviction. MSS members feel the SNA is treating them like amateur cavers who cannot be trusted in Goliath's Cave. Even if the MSS is reading too much into the DNR/SNA's regard for its responsi-bilities, the members feel somewhat disrespected. From their perspective, to think of someone like Dave Gerboth as an am-ateur caver is a little like thinking of Meriwether Lewis as a dabbling frontiersman.

But other members share Gerboth's standards. None of them would venture into a wild cave without a hard hat, am-ple backup batteries, knee pads, and the other equipment re-quired for safe exploration. Not only can members describe the difference between the Stewartville and Dubuque geologic layers, but when exploring underground they can easily identify them. They are also well versed in the nomenclature of cave formations and fossils: soda straws, stalactites, stalagmites, bacon rinds, flowstone, aprons, breakdown, crinoids, and numerous other obscure and esoteric geologic and archeological terms and phrases.

The MSS members try to explain that the rigors of cave exploration—crawling on your belly through mud, gravel, or ice-cold water, scaling or descending underground cliffs, bending and stooping through four-foot-high passages, angling sideways along razor-sharp scalloped walls, and especially the hard, boring work of moving dirt to locate entrances—essentially weed out the careless and casual. These ardent caving enthusiasts should definitely not be considered amateurs. They expend much effort, money, and sometimes blood in the pursuit of exploring the unknown, and without their endeavors the DNR and the rest of the world would not know of Goliath's Cave.

But Djupstrom continues to assert the DNR's perspective. Under no circumstances will any recreational caving be allowed in Goliath's Cave. For the time being, the cave will be permanently gated. Applications for permits will be reviewed by the SNA and/or knowledgeable DNR professionals. Permits will be granted only for scientific purposes.

When an MSS member asks how many permits have been granted to date, Djupstrom tells them "none at this time."

Has anyone entered the cave since it was acquired by the SNA, and is there a list of those who have entered?

Yes, Djupstrom says. The list is on file, but it is a short list.

How is the SNA monitoring the cave?

DNR officials, Djupstrom says, from Forestville/Mystery Cave State Park.

Finally, frustrated, the MSS members want a clear answer for why the cave is off-limits to the public. Why to them, clearly knowledgeable cavers who have educated the DNR/SNA and could assist in its management of the site?

Bob Djupstrom reiterates that the DNR professionals at Mystery Cave are thinking about and exploring the best way to survey and inventory Mystery Cave. They will use that process to create cave survey protocols, and those will then be applied to Goliath's Cave. Once the protocols are in place, the DNR/SNA envisions the MSS members could be part of the scientific effort. Djupstrom re-emphasizes that the work that will be done in Goliath's Cave will never involve recreational caving.

The cave is dangerous, Djupstrom reminds them. It is prone to flooding, and the DNR/SNA worries about liability. Further, the cave will be closed so its fragile environment and its remarkable formations can be protected. He also reminds everyone there are plenty of wild caves in southeastern Minnesota that do not have the same impediments to entry. For the purposes of at least one cave—Goliath's—MSS cavers, Djupstrom asserts, are in the same category as the general public. No exceptions.

Finally, Djupstrom reiterates the permitting process and what it entails. If a permit for scientific purposes is granted, whoever enters the cave will be escorted by a DNR official, either Warren Netherton or Mark White.

Daniel Doctor and Calvin Alexander agree completely on both the need for protection of cave environments and the inherent dangers involved in entering the wild underground. But they also know the value of caving organizations like the

MSS. In fact, MSS members have been particularly helpful to Alexander's fieldwork, as have his students and other non-DNR professionals. Surely there is a better way to protect the cave than by simply locking the entrance and granting access only to particular individuals within the DNR, or to scientists who prove the merit of their need to enter Goliath's Cave through the SNA's bureaucratic permitting process. And the need to be chaperoned by White or Netherton places another unnecessary impediment on entering the cave, one that also consumes the valuable time of DNR professionals charged with an entirely different responsibility—the management and oversight of Forestville/Mystery Cave State Park.

By meeting's end, Doctor and Alexander are as frustrated as the rest of the MSS members. Surveying and inventorying will eventually occur, but not in the foreseeable future. So if MSS members want to enter the cave, they must be conducting scientific research, apply for a permit, and await a careful review.

Calvin Alexander, for one, gets the distinct impression he need not bother to apply. And he is not alone.

For now, unfortunately, it seems as though Goliath's Cave will be indefinitely closed.

15

Drilling

The two-acre parcel formerly of Venita Sikkink's farm, now owned by John Ackerman

November 4, 2004

The late fall day is cool and overcast. The dusting of snow from a week earlier has melted, and now the fallow field under the massive drill rig sits quiet and brown in the metallic light.

John Ackerman looks on as the Thein Well Company sets up in the flat center of Ackerman's recently acquired two-acre parcel. The rig is on the back end of a semitrailer truck. When its bed is elevated, it looks like a mini–missile launcher—at least from a distance. Up close, the drill bit looks like something out of a science fiction movie. The forward digging end is approximately fifteen inches in diameter and is studded with rotating carbide steel drill bits that will hammer and claw through the solid rock. A couple of feet above it, like the petals of a huge deadly flower, another ring of rotating drill bits lines its steel head, thirty inches in diameter. The forward drill grinds and punches the initial hole into the rock, while the second part widens the hole to its full bore. It is all mounted on a long steel shaft designed to support and withstand the heavy pounding the rig is about to endure.

Thein Well Company, the largest well drilling firm in the Upper Midwest, knows exactly where to drill.

Just two weeks earlier, Ackerman hired a quarry drilling rig to punch a four-inch hole through the bedrock to locate the main cave passage linking the eastern side of Goliath's Cave with the part of the cave under the Cherry Grove Blind Valley SNA.

The target was the main cave passage due east of the gravel road and due west of the Side Tributary passage. It is a six- to eight-foot-wide passage estimated to be eight to ten stories underground and over a football field from the cave's natural entrance. He and Dave Gerboth used an old map Gerboth drew back in the mid-1980s, from compass and tape measure readings and from a memory informed by several early visits into the cave. He had a pretty good idea where the cave passage was located, but the method was as much guesswork as carefully measured reckoning. Understandably, their first effort swung wide of the mark. After drilling over one hundred feet, they decided they'd missed the shaft. Truth is, they weren't exactly certain how deep they had to dig because they never had a chance to make any clear depth readings in this part of the cave. Gerboth thought somewhere around eighty feet, but he couldn't be sure. The DNR/SNA policies would not permit them to access the cave's natural entrance to make depth measurements and take compass readings. So they had to try to figure it out on their own.

Their second attempt also swung wide of the mark. They began getting discouraged. But Ackerman was committed to the project.

To say John Ackerman has been disappointed by the SNA's first four years of Goliath's Cave management would be a significant understatement. Ackerman, along with other members of the MSS, were angered by the SNA's refusal to allow entry into the cave except by permit. And the effort to map Mystery Cave, the task to be completed first, was huge and its progress painstakingly slow. Warren Netherton, the DNR cave specialist in charge of heading up the survey, has also been busy building a first-rate Mystery Cave interpretive center and overseeing the day-to-day management of that cave. Everyone agrees his efforts have been nothing short of exceptional, but there is only so much one professional can do.

In the four years since the SNA took over Goliath's Cave, two permits have been granted, only one of which involved entering the cave. Gerda Nordquist, a DNR biologist, applied and received permission to enter Goliath's Cave to conduct a winter bat count. Special Permit Number 2000–2R stated,

> By virtue of the authority conferred on me by the Commissioner of Natural Resources relative to Scientific and Natural Areas, I grant permission to:

> Gerda Nordquist, MCBS [Minnesota County Biological Survey] Animal Survey Coordinator, and two experienced assistants selected from the MCBS staff and under the watchful eye of Cave Specialist, Warren Netherton, Mystery Cave, Forestville State Park,
>
> to enter upon the above Scientific and Natural Area (SNA) including the underground caves and passages with the necessary caving gear and equipment for the purpose of conducting a winter bat survey.

It was signed by Ellen Fuge, SNA staff, for Bob Djupstrom.

Calvin Alexander was one of Nordquist's assistants. Why a highly qualified DNR biologist who was also a caver, with Calvin Alexander and at least one other person, needed to be overseen by "the watchful eye" of the DNR's Netherton is unclear, maybe even a little absurd—at least from the perspective of Alexander, Ackerman, Gerboth, and fellow MSS cavers. They feel it demonstrates the lack of trust between the MSS and the DNR and the almost paranoiac oversight of the cave by the SNA. Either that or an institutional sense of humor.

Unfortunately, Nordquist and her colleagues found no bats in the cave, and so their effort ended after their first visit. Since that time, the only other permit granted for the Cherry Grove Blind Valley SNA was to Calvin Alexander and Jeff Green, DNR hydrologist, to conduct a dye trace on the surface of the site.

Alexander doesn't believe any permit he submitted that involved doing research inside Goliath's Cave, regardless of its scientific merits, would be approved.

Finally, on the third attempt, the quarry drilling rig broke into open passage. Ackerman and Gerboth were pleased. But it wasn't until Gerboth rigged up a narrow video camera to a long cable feed and lowered it, with a tape measure, seventy-five feet through the narrow passage, that they were sure their effort was successful and they knew the shaft's exact length. What they saw in the camera's small monitor couldn't have looked better. Turn the lens 360 degrees, and you could see they were near the center of the central cave passage, exactly where they wanted to be.

Now the Thein Well Company's foreman readies the heavy bit to enter the ground just a few feet to the side of the quarry drill's small hole. The well rig will drill a thirty-inch-wide chute to the side of the original hole; this will prevent the debris from falling into the smaller shaft and filling up the cave passage. They can drill just short of the cave, make sure the shaft is clear of debris, and then drill the last few inches. The drill will not overshoot its mark, and when it finally breaks through there will be less damage to the cave and less rock and debris cleanup.

The drill is positioned, a complex of stabilizers are put into place, and finally the heavy engine kicks in, and the steel teeth at the end of the thick steel shaft drop and pound into the earth.

The sound thunders across the dark brown stubble of the field and the nearby rolling hills and the Cherry Grove Blind Valley SNA woods across the gravel road. It is like standing beside a gigantic jackhammer, with tons of pressure behind every three-inch rise and punch. You can feel the percussive hit. After watching the complex drill bit pound into the ground and then slowly rise up and pound again, twisting as it rises and drops, they finally hear it hit solid bedrock. The pound and grind ratchets up another decibel, and the downward progress of the huge drill bit slows.

Drilling a hole this large can be a complicated, painstaking process. But it is mesmerizing to watch the massive machinery do its work.

Ackerman cannot help but smile. He begins to recall the line from the Grateful Dead song: "What a long, strange trip it's been." In spite of the din, he can hear the song playing in his head.

Ever since Ron Spong entered Goliath's Cave in 1980, it has been problematic to explore. The second sump, approximately 175 feet into the main entrance, fills with water most of the year. Jim Magnusson and his volunteers made long and difficult efforts to dig a second entrance into the site. Just two feet short, at a depth of about twenty-one feet, Magnusson's hopes were dashed when Tom Kappers ceased to allow caving activities of any kind on his property.

Ackerman watches the drill do its work. This time, that second entrance will finally be realized.

For four years, Goliath's Cave has been closed to recreational cavers. Alexander and Doctor, two of the scientists among the MSS membership, have not applied to perform any scientific research on the site because they do not believe they will get permits. Members who lack scientific credentials cannot even apply. Suggestions that the MSS and others work on mapping the cave fell on deaf ears.

John Ackerman doesn't appreciate government interference. Truth is, he has had his share of conflicts with other caving organizations and cavers in the past, and most especially with the DNR. Ackerman knows the measures he takes to open up caves are controversial. Not everyone agrees with dynamiting or drilling their way into caves to which nature has refused easy access.

But for Ackerman, all the conflict and controversy are worth what they let him do: discover, open up, and walk through cave no one has ever before seen. Ackerman loves to be the first. And he has done more virgin exploration than all but a handful of cavers living today.

At this point, John Ackerman's Karst Preserve has two cavern complexes under lock and key. Not that he would ever preclude knowledgeable cavers from entering them. Blasting entryways into his Spring Valley Caverns, in the 1990s, was controversial, but he owned much of the land under which the complex of caves spread, and he acquired caving rights to the land he didn't own outright. In northeast Iowa, where the state had been unable to pay for developing Cold Water Cave (now over seventeen miles long), the tunnel and cave rights reverted to the landowner. Ackerman felt the entrance was being unfairly controlled, so in 2003 he purchased five acres of farmland over one of the passages and caving rights to two hundred acres of adjoining land, then hired Thein to drill a 188-foot-deep vertical shaft into the cave.

Getting continued access to Mystery Cave, now that he thinks of it, was another one of those DNR disappointments. When it was in private hands, before 1989, he and Dave Gerboth and other MSS cavers actually had keys to its entrance. But once the DNR took control, they more or less locked out the two cavers, as well as others in the MSS—at least for a while. Not all of them, but many, as DNR staff sought to understand what it was they owned and how best to manage it. It was particularly frustrating because the MSS had lobbied the legislature on the DNR's behalf.

But Ackerman knows it is part of the complicated story of DNR cave management that not everyone was or has been locked out of Mystery Cave. Prior to the DNR's acquisition of Mystery Cave, Calvin Alexander managed the first good survey of the cave, spending many weekends exploring and surveying the 12.5-mile complex. In fact, Alexander has appreciated how, over the years, Mystery Cave has been opened to sport caving, at reasonable times and under reasonable conditions. Scientific research in the cave has also proceeded with encouragement and assistance from the staff. And educational trips with students, Alexander found, have actually become routine.

But their experience with the SNA's management of Goliath's Cave has been very different. After four years of waiting for the DNR/SNA to loosen its steel grip, Ackerman thought he had a better idea. It has long been known that much of the system ran under the adjacent farm. One day in the spring of this year, he visited its ninety-one-year-old owner, Venita Sikkink. What he encountered surprised and pleased him.

Sikkink still lived alone on her farm. She attributed her remarkable good health, in part, to the water flowing through Goliath's Cave directly under her property and into her farmhouse well. More or less a kindred spirit, she was disappointed that Goliath's Cave had been closed off to exploration and scientific research.

Ackerman suggested Goliath's Cave could be opened again, with a year-round entrance. If Mrs. Sikkink sold him a couple of surface acres directly over the main cave passage coming out of the SNA's land, he would sink a hole into it, and exploration and scientific research could finally resume.

Sikkink wasn't sure. She turned to the rest of her family, and Ackerman met her oldest son and some of the other Sikkinks. To demonstrate that he was serious about his proposal and his commitment to opening up caves, he invited the entire family to his Spring Valley Caverns site. The Sikkinks toured the cave and were impressed by the facility Ackerman built at the site to act as an entryway to the massive cave system.

Finally, Mrs. Sikkink was convinced. She sold Ackerman the two acres at the western end of her land and all the subsurface caving rights to it. And another step was taken on the *long, strange trip* to what was happening before him right now, in the cool midmorning of this late fall day.

* * *

The Sikkink family tours Spring Valley Caverns, 2004. Venita Sikkink is seated, fourth from left; John Ackerman is standing, fourth from right. Courtesy John Ackerman

The complex drill bit continues eating into the bedrock. It rises three inches, drops with a massive hammer, twists as it hits the ground, pulverizes, crushes, and crumples just an inch or two of stone, and then rises to repeat the process. Again and again. Its hammering is only paused by the periodic cleaning out of the rock it has loosened. The drill bit hammers, turns, and grinds, and the solid stone gradually gives way.

Of course, once the DNR and the greater public found out about Ackerman's purchase and intent, it is fair to say all hell broke loose. He watches the drill continue in its work and recalls the way people both in the DNR and outside it tried to stop him. But this wasn't the first time Ackerman had acquired land and opened up pristine cave using a drill bit and explosives. And it wouldn't be his last, he'd guess, if he was a betting man.

Ackerman knows there are many who disagree with his methods. Warren Netherton and Mark White, the DNR's two cave specialists, and just about everyone else in the DNR and SNA, were absolutely opposed to his efforts here and elsewhere—as are some fellow MSS members. Wet, wild caves like Goliath's are often impassable, they argue. That's simply the nature of wild caves in karst regions. That doesn't mean we should dig, drill, or blast a new entry into wild places. You might as well build a road into the Boundary Waters Canoe Area.

But Ackerman's perspective is entirely different. If you cannot get into a cave to explore it or perform scientific research in it, then it is not being accessed, studied, or used. And in any case, he is not paving a pathway *in* the pristine cave. Above all else he is a cave preservationist and conservationist.

He is only creating an *entry* into the cave—one that can be gated, locked, and used year-round. To use Netherton's and White's analogy, it is like building a road up to the edge of the Boundary Waters. Like the Gunflint Trail, Ackerman muses. That's what he is doing here. He's making a trail through the limestone bedrock up to the cave's perimeter. Perhaps he should call it the Limestone Trail. The idea makes him realize he needs to come up with a good name for this new, permanent entryway into Goliath's Cave.

After the Thein Well Company finishes its work here, and after the cleanup of the site is completed, a steel culvert will be inserted into the hole and a steel lid with a lock will be welded to the top of it. Then exploration, discovery, and research at Goliath's can again continue. And no one will have to complete a permit application or be subject to DNR or SNA whims in order to enter it.

Calvin Alexander has appreciated John Ackerman's efforts, here and elsewhere. Given the nearly complete lack of entry or activity in Goliath's Cave over the previous four years, he suspected it would be a long time before exploration or research at Goliath's Cave would continue.

Alexander's friendship with Ackerman has created some problems for the professor. But the relationship has given the scientist access to more miles of wild cave than the vast majority of his colleagues. And he has used that access to do research.

Had the SNA allowed it, the professor believes he could have put together an excellent group of volunteers to keep the natural entrance to Goliath's Cave cleared of plant matter and debris. In the previous four years, he could have begun or even completed a survey and inventory of the entire site, as he had been doing at Mystery Cave. During that time, he would have also performed some hydrogeological research in the cave. He would like to place water sensors throughout the cave, to register water volume and flow through the year, tracking periods of rainfall and snowmelt. He would also like to test water purity throughout different parts of the cave and at different times.

Alexander supported the idea of this year-round entrance into Goliath's from the beginning. He had even lobbied the DNR and SNA to create a second entrance, although he knew the idea was anathema to them. And it isn't only the DNR who disagrees with Ackerman's methods. Some cavers from other organizations, most notably the Wisconsin and Iowa grottos of the National Speleological Society, have been angered by the drilling, especially at Cold Water Cave in Iowa. Even some members of the Minnesota grotto have taken issue, which might be one of the reasons Ackerman never attends their monthly meetings (though he is still active in the membership).

But Ackerman is not the first to drill an entrance into a cave system. In fact, the state of Iowa drilled the first entrance into Cold Water long before Ackerman sunk his entrance. And many people drill wells into karst caves— so many, in fact, that guidelines have been published about how to safely drill into a karst cave system, lining, caulking, and capping the new entryway.

Daniel Doctor, one in a distinguished line of Alexander's doctoral students, also disagreed with some of Ackerman's cave opening methods. He would never have drilled another entrance into Goliath's Cave. There is no doubt in his mind that the process alters the cave's ecology by creating another source of air entering the cave. In addition, if the entrance is not sealed correctly, or if the overhead bedrock is unstable, it could damage the cave.

On October 11, 2004, Alexander sent an e-mail discussing the problems of Goliath's entrance to Jeff Green, DNR hydrologist, with copies to Mark White and Gerda Nordquist. He reviewed the dangers of the natural entrance and Jim Magnusson's efforts to dig a new one, suggesting that a safe, new entryway "was and is an important step in any rational investigation and study of the portion of Goliath under the SNA. Construction of such a new entrance would be an easy afternoon's work for John, his caver friends and the 'Cave Finder' track hoe. It could be accomplished at no cost to the DNR."

In addition, Alexander pointed out that, because of the difficult crawl between the cave's two main sections,

> Any reasonably safe access to the portion of Goliath under Mrs. Sikkink's land requires a new entrance in the large, downstream Canyon Section outside of the SNA. That is what John currently plans to construct. His effort would be simplified if he were permitted to take his cave radio into the SNA portion of Goliath, through the low wet crawl and into Canyon Section of Goliath to locate the precise spot on the surface to drill a new entrance. He can and will construct the entrance without such permission—as he clearly has the legal and ethical right to do. Such cooperation on the DNR's part, however, could be the start of establishing a productive co-equal management of the Goliath Cave System by its two legal owners.

> My advice to John was to see if the permit system described on the Cherry Grove Blind Valley SNA web page actually works. He seemed to be willing to do so yesterday. I think it is impor-

tant, however, to remind the DNR that John has a very limited tolerance of bureaucratic roadblocks or delays.

As a karst hydrogeologist and as a caver it is my sincere hope that the two owners of Goliath can establish a productive, co-equal management effort that will simultaneously protect the cave and make it safe for reasonable scientific investigation and for recreational use. This e-mail is meant to be a step in that direction.

John Ackerman never applied for a permit because he didn't believe one should be required. Instead, his letter of October 14, 2004, explained why he believes the SNA should allow him entry through the natural entrance. He recounts some of the cave's history, including his own effort to purchase the site from the Kapperses when the DNR was negotiating for it. Once the DNR acquired the site, he notes, he felt pleased: "Good . . . 1999 will be a great year –the cave will be permanently protected and we will once again have access." His letter continues,

> Instead, imagine how shocked we were when the SNA snubbed us like Lepers. Correct me if I am wrong, but I know of only a couple of trips that have taken place since the SNA purchased the cave. (A key DNR employee was required to escort the visitors) I have been informed since then by various DNR personnel that no matter what the SNA website states, this cave is totally off limits and will never be open to visitation. In fact, your personal meeting with the Minnesota Speleological Survey in July 2001 unequivocally confirmed this. . . .
>
> How ironic that the property was purchased specifically because of the cave, but even the qualified seasoned cavers who discovered, protected and mapped it are banned from seeing it! The numerous entrance signs surrounding the site even spell it out! How shameful that our tax dollars were spent on such a purchase just to keep us from entering it.
>
> I (The Minnesota Karst Preserve) have purchased land over the cave system so exploration and scientific research can once

again resume. I now own property over the cave and the underground rights to all of Venita Sikkink's property. The DNR and the Minnesota Karst Preserve now jointly own Goliath Cave. This event occurred due to the direct support from the landowner and many constituents.

I ask that you reconsider your past regulations and consider to allow limited access through the publicly funded gated SNA entrance. I do not need this right of entry to accomplish the new cave entrance; this will be done using the map we drafted shortly after the caves discovery—along with other aids. I simply ask that you allow limited access to the SNA portion of Goliath's Cave to qualified competent cavers and scientists for other obvious reasons that we can discuss in the near future.

I (and a large support group) would like to work with the DNR/SNA staff to establish a mutually beneficial enduring relationship so this cave system can be safely visited to enhance exploratory and scientific knowledge.

The rig's engine chuffs and drones as it raises the huge carbide steel bit, then hammers it into the bedrock. Ackerman can feel it in his feet and up through his legs. The drill bit is doing its work. Bit by bit, no pun intended, he thinks. Eventually, a new entrance will be cut, lined, sealed, and locked.

It took Thein a few months to drill the 188-foot hole into Cold Water Cave. This one will be less involved, because it is only seventy-five feet.

Bob Djupstrom hasn't yet responded to Ackerman's letter. But he's not worried about it. That's how large, monolithic bureaucracies work, and that's what he hates about them. There is no answer from a single person. Everything happens by committee. Eventually, he guesses, he will get a response. And technically it will come from Djupstrom. But by then, he suspects the Thein Well Company's work will be done and he will have already started his explorations of this section of Goliath's Cave.

He turns to the foreman and smiles. "Looks good!" he yells over the sound of the engine.

The foreman smiles back. "We'll get there."

John nods. "I'll be back and check in a couple days," he says.

"We'll be here." The foreman knows it will be a long job.

Then Ackerman turns and starts off through the stubble field, walking toward his cream-colored Ackerman's Furniture van. He starts mulling a proper name for his entrance. He thinks he has an idea.

His thoughts drift to the undiscovered country underground. Not long, now, and he will be able to see the fabled Rubicon passage and find new territory in a cave system he feels certain has more secrets to reveal.

16
David's Entrance
John Ackerman's two-acre parcel at Jessie's Grove
Wednesday, December 1, 2004

The sky shows a solid bank of clouds and the temperature hovers just below freezing. A thin dusting of snow coats the fields that roll to the eastern horizon. To the west, only a matter of yards, cuts the gravel road that separates John Ackerman's new addition to the Karst Preserve from the DNR's Cherry Grove Blind Valley SNA.

The ground is hard, and in parts the light snow is crusted and icy. Ackerman, Clay Kraus, and Dave Gerboth are dressed for the cold. By the end of the afternoon Ackerman suspects he will be shedding a layer or two. Seventy-five feet down, through this recently completed chute, one of Goliath's main passages maintains its perpetual 47 degrees. It won't be easy getting to it, and the work he must do will be exhausting. By the end of the day he figures he will be tired, hot, and sweaty.

But Ackerman grins. Christmas is coming early. For several years he has wanted to return to Goliath's Cave. And for several years he has not been alone. Plenty of others agree with his efforts to open up a second entrance into Goliath's, and now he can—though much, much work remains to be done.

After twenty-six days of intermittent drilling, the Thein Well Company finally stopped just inches short of the final punch into the cave passage. Drilling a normal well, on a site like this, they would not be so concerned about clearing the rock and debris as they drilled. But they have worked with Ackerman before, and they know he is particular about how to proceed—which is just one of the reasons the job that they expected to take a few days has taken a little longer.

Finally yesterday, Ackerman received the call. The shaft was clear all the way down to the final few inches. They would punch the hole later that day. Then they would line the top part of the shaft with a cylindrical metal culvert and seal off the edges of the culvert with cement. They would place a temporary cover over it. Once it was done, Ackerman knew he would have to go down and clear the final pieces of stone from the cave's passage. But since no one, to the best of his knowledge, had been in this part of the cave in at least four years, probably more like the last decade, he was looking forward to the work.

Last night, he was so excited sleep came slowly. It was like being a boy again.

Now he lifts off the temporary cover and peers down the clean, cylindrical shaft to where it disappears into darkness. He and Gerboth stake down and secure the line. Then they drop the rope into the hole, and Ackerman, who is a technical rock climber, carefully drops over the shaft's lip and starts rappelling into darkness.

On his slow descent, it is easy to keep himself centered. Using his back, hands, and knees, he could actually brace himself against the sides and come to a full, hovering stop. But he is anxious to get to the bottom and continues to rappel.

Halfway down, he examines the perfectly round, vertical chute. He is amazed by the well driller's work. Thein Well Company deserves every cent of the high cost of drilling this well. The shaft is a thing of engineering beauty. As far as the sunlight reaches, the smooth surface of the rock is clean, and in places the bedrock sparkles with tiny particles of quartz.

Dropping seventy-five feet on a rope is an arduous exercise. His gloved hands grip the rope. Farther down into the shaft, Ackerman must rely on his headlamp to view the smooth stone sides. Finally, after a few minutes, his feet swing into the main cave passage, and he drops to the pebbly bottom.

There is fresh debris here, but surprisingly little. Peering up into the shaft, he yells to Gerboth.

"Ready for the bucket! Lower it down!" Then he steps to the side and begins to examine the passage into which he has dropped.

Ackerman is stunned. It is large and spacious and appears to run on forever into the darkness in both an easterly and westerly direction. Its walls are a little uneven, but otherwise it is almost as though the passage has been chiseled by an engineer, almost as though the Thein Well Company has been down here working.

While Ackerman awaits the bucket, he spends a few minutes walking into the darkness of Goliath's Cave, along this passage only a handful of people have ever seen. He feels the emotion of it in the top center of his chest, a tightness and intensity he will not soon forget. He longs to move off and continue walking into darkness.

But for now, there is much work to be done.

"Got it?" Gerboth yells down the shaft.

Ackerman returns to where the bucket sits on a pile of rubble. "Got it," he yells up the opening, his voice echoing off into the cave's darkness. And then he starts filling the bucket with stone.

On November 15 or 16, two weeks after Thein Well Company began drilling, Calvin Alexander calls Bob Djupstrom with a request to go through Goliath's natural entrance in January 2005 to obtain a soil sample from a dry part of the cave floor and check it for nitrates, as he has already done in Mystery Cave, Niagara Cave, and Crystal Cave. Djupstrom e-mails him the application form and makes a record of the call in the Cherry Grove Blind Valley file on November 18, 2004. Djupstrom notes that he talked with Mark White about the call, and they shared their suspicions that Alexander "was probably looking to GPS locations for Ackerman." They discussed alternatives to the permit—having a DNR employee collect the dirt, or suggesting that Alexander sample Coon Cave instead. Djupstrom asks if White or Warren Netherton could accompany Alexander, and White agrees, "though Calvin wouldn't like it. . . . We would only allow Calvin to take in a trowel and plastic bag; no other equipment to preclude other things from taking place."

Since the new shaft had already been started, it is unclear how GPS coordinates would have helped Ackerman. But the SNA's concern for controlling access to Goliath's Cave and keeping the site pristine continues unchanged.

* * *

A workman welds the steel rotation device in place. Courtesy John Ackerman

Through the rest of December and into the New Year, work continues on the new entrance. Not long after the cavers clear out the debris, they affix a steel head to the top of the shaft and then weld on a removable steel plate and put a lock on it.

The news of the drilling continues to move through the caving community like a mild shock wave. Dawn Ryan, president of the Wisconsin Speleological Society, adamantly opposes the maverick caver's methods, and she had protested vociferously when he drilled the new entrance into Cold Water Cave. On December 1, 2004, she calls the SNA "to discuss the urgency of inventorying the Goliath Cave since the new entrance was created," according to an unsigned note in the file. She suggests that she and John Lovaas, science director of Cold Water Cave in Iowa, might assist in making the inventory.

Djupstrom and White discuss the idea, which Djupstrom notes "would ensure we know what is there, where it is at, what condition it is in, and serve as a baseline. Though everyone I have spoken with doesn't think Ackerman will intentionally damage features in the state portion of Goliath cave it is fair to say they feel he would enlarge small openings in order to gain access. This kind of damage can't be tolerated in the state cave."

White and Djupstrom also discuss the three approaches to cave mapping: a "go anywhere approach and do your own thing," a "survey without mapping" (presumably to identify and document the primary geologic formations in the cave), and "the NPS [National Park Service] approach which is map and do a careful survey and inventory as you go. This is the conservative, go slow, be thorough approach." White recommends the NPS approach, which requires training the mappers. Djupstrom agrees, noting that White and Warren Netherton are planning on training people this coming February, to finally conduct a survey and inventory of Mystery Cave. The note continues,

> Mark suggested that in light of our need now that perhaps the training could focus on the "Commercial part of Mystery" then Goliath next. This would postpone survey of his other portions of Mystery until later. I told him I was inclined to involve the Wis. and Iowa folks in this effort; they were the only ones to come forth. I told Mark we could assist in funding for it if needed.
>
> Mark noted that MSS members have done the work at Mystery to date. He is a little concerned that to not have MSS members but Iowa and Wisconsin cave experts map and inventory Goliath would be seen as a slam. I noted that the only members of the caving community to approach us and express concern over the new entrance has been the outside interests i.e. Wisconsin and Iowa. They apparently are not intimidated by Ackerman. I agreed that I do share the concern about not involving the MSS however as we want to ensure they are not excluded but brought into the process. There is the trust factor among that membership right now. Right now if Ackerman showed up we would not want him in there.

On December 29, 2004, Ackerman finally receives Djupstrom's response to his mid-October letter. The letter is largely a formal recitation of the SNA's purpose, particularly with regard to Goliath's Cave. Djupstrom mentions the need to preserve the site and its value to the SNA. As he had explained at the July 2001 meeting with the MSS, Goliath will not be mapped until Mystery Cave is mapped and proper protocol has been created. That process, he says, is just beginning.

Djupstrom confirms that there has been just one visit to

Goliath's Cave, Gerda Nordquist's winter bat count in February 2000, since the SNA acquired its only wild entrance. Finally, he concludes,

> In response to your comment that the DNR and yourself now jointly own the Goliath Cave, please be informed that entry into the underground portions of the state land i.e. Cherry Grove Blind Valley SNA, continues to be illegal without a permit. The Department of Natural Resources through the Scientific and Natural Areas Program, remains committed to protecting this unique and sensitive geological resource. The current DNR regulations ensure that this will take place on the state property, both above and below ground.
>
> Should the DNR receive a request to conduct scientific research that will assist the DNR in protecting and managing this resource we would be happy to take it under consideration. As was noted at the July 2001 meeting with the MSS, we envision a working relationship wherein qualified cavers including MSS members may assist in carrying out research under the guidance of DNR personnel

Entering Goliath's Cave through the new entrance is not particularly easy, even with a chain ladder dropped over its edge. Clay Kraus creates a solid metal ladder, which they drop into the hole in sections and painstakingly bolt to the wall. The firm ladder makes entering and exiting the cave a little easier.

In January 2005, Gerboth, Kraus, and Ackerman systematically scour the non-SNA portions of the cave for unknown passages and select promising sites for further exploration. After removing sediment from three sites, they squirm through the constrictions to find major new cave segments. They lay plans to explore two very promising leads. One is at the end of the Side Tributary passage: a sump that requires a dive with scuba gear in order to determine if the underwater passage leads to new cave. Others have tried to snorkel through it, but it is too deep. Still, the passage has always appeared relatively wide and spacious—at least by Minnesota caving standards.

They have also hiked to the end of the Rubicon passage. They feel pretty certain that with a little additional pushing they might be able to uncover one or two additional leads, perhaps beyond the waterfall or near the ceiling, over a hundred feet up, which will take them into extensive new cave.

Finally, Ackerman is ready to christen his new entrance. He and Clay Kraus drive down to place the sign on the western entrance to his property.

After all his efforts—negotiations and land purchase, drilling to locate the passage, drilling the entrance, constructing the locked entrance and the ladder—Ackerman's incendiary sense of humor kicks in. In honor of the biblical story in which David slew Goliath, he will call it *David's Entrance.*

The sign placement further makes the point. On the Cherry Grove Blind Valley SNA side of the road, a DNR sign marks the area and an SNA sign lists the rules:

> This area was established to protect and perpetuate Minnesota's rare and unique natural resources for nature observation, education and research purposes.
>
> Principle activities which are UNLAWFUL in the use of this area are listed below:
> - Collecting plants, animals, rocks and fossils
> - Camping, picnicking and swimming
> - Horses, dogs and other pets
> - Snowmobiles and other unauthorized vehicles
> - Hunting, trapping, fishing and boating

· A written permit from the Commissioner of Natural Resources is required to enter any portion of this site below ground.

It is illegal for any person to possess on their person any caving equipment, shovel, pry bar, hammer, torch or other tool or instrument that could be used to damage or move stone, soil or the subsurface while on this site without a written permit from the Commissioner of Natural Resources.

Directly across the road, Ackerman posts two signs of his own. The first is an official-looking red, white, and blue emblem declaring the location to be part of the MINNESOTA KARST PRESERVE. The second lists some of John Ackerman's rules for the site.

Goliath's Cave Site
"David's Entrance"

This area was established to protect and perpetuate Minnesota's rare and unique natural underground resources for natural observation, education and research purposes.

In 1999 a division of the DNR (Scientific Natural Area) purchased the parcel just west of this site that contains the natural entrance to Goliath's Cave. A gate was subsequently installed to prevent entry to the cave system.

As a result, a second entrance was created 160 feet northeast of here on private land and is now included as part of the Minnesota Karst Preserve. Entry inquiries can be forwarded to www.karstpreserve.com

17
Sump Diving
Goliath's Cave, end of the Side Tributary passage
  and beyond
October 29, 2005

On April 29, 2001, John Ackerman almost died while scuba diving into an underground spring. The potential cave was approximately twenty miles southeast of Goliath's, on the Minnesota-Iowa border near the town of Granger. Deep underground, the silt turned the water into a black cloud and he became hopelessly entangled in his dive line, like a fly in a spider web. But he lived to tell the story, swearing he would never again attempt cave diving. It was a type of underground exploration better left to the experts.

That doesn't mean, though, that Ackerman will stop. His obsession is becoming well known: in September, he learned that he will be featured as one of the top ten "Adventurers of 2005" in the December 2005/January 2006 issue of *National Geographic Adventure Magazine*. The magazine divides the list into Elites and Iconoclasts—and Ackerman is the first Iconoclast to be listed.

Now he leads a group of eight down the main trunk line of Goliath's Cave, hauling scuba gear toward the narrow sump at the end of the Side Tributary. This particular sump looks unremarkable, the kind of small pond many people install in their backyards and surround with decorative stone. If you approach carefully, you can peer into its crystalline depths. But the pool, like the rabbit hole in *Alice in Wonderland,* appears to go on forever—or at least to somewhere deep, unknown, and potentially dangerous.

Ever since Ackerman first eyed this sump, he has believed it was the doorway to an extensive cave system. Not the Odessa system, the thirty-mile cave system for which he has searched in the past. But certainly some additional, big, dramatic cave passage. Surface debris— the old tire or a wayward tin can or shoe—provided the clues. The occasional floods that deluge the area wash junk into the sinkholes and flush it into these underground passages. There are at least two sinkholes in the woods overhead, and Ackerman feels certain that one of those passages lies beyond this sump. The nearest sinkhole sits in what is now Cherry Grove, a small acreage of nearby woods. Other sinkholes are spread out and, he guesses, quite far from this sump, which means the cave system beyond this watery entryway could be very, very large.

But someone has to risk his life to find out. Ackerman had sworn it would never be he, but the sump exerts a strong attraction on the monomaniacal cave explorer. Lately he has wondered if he should reconsider his moratorium.

Then, in a timely coincidence, Ackerman received an e-mail from John Preston, an NSS–CDS (National Speleological Society–Cave Diving Section) certified cave diver now living in Rochester, Minnesota. Preston was looking for some Minnesota caves he might be able to probe in scuba gear. Ackerman

Sump at the end of the Side Tributary, Goliath's Cave, before John Preston's dive line was attached to a formation along its left wall. Courtesy John Ackerman

told him he had just the place. In the past four months, they have made two unsuccessful tries. But today will be different.

The team of eight includes four experienced cavers—Ackerman, Dave Gerboth, Charlie Graling, and Clay Kraus—who are familiar with this passage and the grueling effort it takes to get here. Preston has been here before but still can't get used to the haul. It is the first trip for Preston's three cave-diving friends, Dave Owen, Roger Southwick, and Alex Carlson, all from the Rochester area. They have heard stories about this trek, but hearing it is somewhat different from walking it step by step.

First they descend the narrow seventy-five-foot shaft. When you are fully geared up for a normal exploration, the climb down the ladder is difficult. When you are planning to dive a sump and, you hope, to explore sections of underground passage no one has ever seen and whose length is unknown, and you want to live to tell the story, prudence dictates you equip yourself for the unexpected. The burden of your haul increases five-fold.

Next they slog through a main trunk line passage to the Side Tributary, which runs for over six hundred difficult feet. At times they are up to their waists in water. The narrow walls can be sharp edged and unforgiving. At other times they bend sideways, inching forward step by step with tanks and equipment held away from their bodies. Their shoulders ache, their arms feel ready to fall off, and by the time Preston reaches the V chamber, a twenty-foot-long, six-foot-wide passage in front of the crystal-clear pool, he is ready to take a dip just to cool down.

* * *

Preston believes he knows what he is getting into. At five feet eleven inches and 210 pounds, with legs like a pair of tree trunks, he can hold his own in any tight crevasse. But strength is no match for eighty feet of bedrock and blackout conditions. What cave divers need more than physical strength is steel nerve. They need to be able to assert reason and sanity in situations that would send normal human beings to an early grave.

One of the keys to today's successful effort, Preston knows, is water clarity. On his two previous attempts, he learned that the pool of water ran deep and was wide enough to dive but that it silted in faster than a sirocco across a desert dune. Moments after entering the sump, he was dead blind. He could not see where he was, what lay ahead, or any of the possible openings he might be able to probe to emerge into a new cave passage—let alone his depth or pressure gauges, or his hand in front of his face. He was able to exit the cave using one of the most important skills of cave diving: maintaining his dive reel line so he did not become entangled in the connection that was his only way back to the surface.

Today, all of the men in this group can sense something different is about to happen. They hope it isn't tragedy. In spite of the dangers, Preston keeps diving these sumps because he says it gives him chills to think he will be the first person to set foot in pristine cave, where very likely no other human has been.

The entourage that accompanies the eminent cave diver is experienced, well prepared, and interested. Ackerman is impressed. And in spite of his promise to his family and himself never to dive another cave sump, he cannot help but be caught up in this excursion. A part of him wishes he were diving, too. It isn't the dive itself that excites him. If he thinks about those dark passages, he has a completely different feeling, one suffused with anxiety, maybe even terror. What compels Ackerman to even consider another flirt with cold, dark, wet death is what lies beyond.

The V chamber preceding the sump is approximately twenty feet long and six feet wide. It is not a comfortable place to prepare, but this time they are all careful to stay well away from the stream that makes a slow exit out of the sump. They want that water to remain crystal clear. And that is what Preston knows will be different about this dive. He is going to make sure the water stays clear.

He suits up at the back of the opening. The other team members shine their lights so it is relatively easy to prepare in the cave. But the headlamps and hand lamps can penetrate only so far. Shadows play across the space.

He affixes his forty-cubic-foot tanks—he's taking two—to his side harness, one on each side, as well as the standard three scout lights, one for the trip and two for backup. In dry caving or cave diving, you always bring three light sources. He then takes hold of his dive reel, double-checks his regulators, weight belt, mask, and bellows bag, and gets ready to cross the ten feet of open water to the edge of the sump.

First they review their communications. Radio and other devices will not penetrate ten feet of solid rock. If Preston reaches into cave that lies beyond the sump, they will have to rely on primitive rope signals.

Dave Owen, who holds the signal rope, works with the Fillmore county dive team and is experienced with line communication. He can tell the difference between just moving around and an actual signal.

"Let's have three signals," Preston suggests.

"Works for me," Owen answers. "How about two pulls if you make it into something, but it isn't worth going any farther and you're coming back?"

Preston thinks about it. "Yeah, that'll work. Hopefully, I won't be using that signal."

They smile in the dark.

"Three pulls, I found a decent air space and start the clock for one hour, so I can look around."

Owen nods.

"And how about four good yanks if I found a huge area. That will also signal the start of a one-hour exploration."

"Sounds good."

They all nod in the dark, hoping for four solid yanks.

Finally, Preston moves to the front edge of the sump. He bends down and uses his mask to peer beneath the surface. He looks twenty feet down toward an angled, boulder-strewn corridor he remembers only by feel from his previous blind dives. The water is incredibly clear.

"Wow," he says, turning to the others assembled near the back of the opening. "It's perfect."

This time, after he steps into the pool, he will turn and dive headfirst, so he can keep his vision in front of the silt.

Preston carefully lets himself over the edge and in a moment is submerged almost to his shoulders. He begins to play out his dive line, getting ready to hand one end to Owen. He pulls on the dive reel, and it suddenly jams. Preston curses in the darkness. The dive reel is the only piece of equipment he has not checked since a recent cave dive in Florida. To enter the sump without the reel would be suicide.

He curses again in the darkness.

And then Owen suggests he use his backup finger spool, a smaller dive reel with only fifty to sixty feet of line. It could work. They hurriedly exchange spools. He is trying to keep his movement to a minimum, but the pool is already starting to cloud. The gentle flow coming out of the sump will not keep the cloud at bay for long.

He makes one quick wave and drops beneath the surface. The water beneath him is still crystal clear. He holds his scout light in front of him, angling it down the corridor. Perfect! He peers down the rocky tunnel and recognizes a few stones he knew only by feel. He is surprised by the corridor's underwater dimensions, how small and tight it appears. At the bottom, at the end of a small channel, he sees a wall with dark space above it. It must be the vertical passage, the fracture into which he tried to ascend on an earlier dive. On that dive he rose in total darkness, by feel, and the fracture became narrower and narrower and finally his tank became wedged into the constrictive rise. But he felt nothing above him except more tight space.

Now he holds his underwater scout light in one hand and pushes into the passage, keeping just ahead of the silt. He can feel the edges of the cloud begin to envelop him. He hopes he can peer into that vertical fracture. He hopes it opens into airy cave, but he has his doubts.

Before reaching the fracture, he peers across the small underwater space. To his right, across a small passage, is an ominous three-foot-wide opening into a dark hole. The prospect of having to enter that dark space makes his heart lurch. He hopes his real break will happen in this fracture.

Finally, he positions himself directly beneath the vertical cavity. He shines his scout light up into the vertical rise and finds . . . nothing but a solid black ceiling of jagged-edged rock. Damn!

The silt is catching up with him. If he is going to enter that dark hole, he had better do it quick. He crosses the small space, trying to manage his breath. As he approaches, he sees the dark hole has a sandy bottom. He is careful about his entry. In ocean diving, a moray eel would likely call this tight space home. But Minnesota's subterranean waters are too damn cold, dark, and deep to support any other life but an occasional fish (providing the underground water is connected to an open surface stream). What he worries about is getting stuck or cut on the tunnel's sharp edges. He pushes forward across the narrow, sandy bottom. He pushes a few more feet, shining his light. He travels about ten feet before he hears something. There is a vertical opening up ahead, and he is sure he hears something. He pushes closer, and he thinks he hears the *drum-drum-drumming* of falling water! He peers up into this vertical fracture, and this time he is stunned. Twelve feet above him, the entire ceiling is a reflecting mirror, a surface broken at one end by a cascade of falling water. He is too astonished to register shock. If the water is falling, it means there is space above it. And though the mirrored surface is not wide—it actually narrows as it climbs—it is wide enough.

Preston's exhale is ecstatic. He carefully follows the bubbles up into the narrowing fracture. He peers at the mirrored surface, moves out from under the falling water, and stops just short of breaking into whatever lies above. It would be foolhardy to push his head into the space without first testing it. If the ceiling is only inches above the surface and he rose quickly, he could knock himself out or jab his head into a stalactite. If you want to survive in underwater caves, caution must guide every decision, every move. He pauses, reaches his gloved hand into the mirror, and touches . . . nothing. He reaches farther and touches . . . nothing. He stretches into the opening, moving from side to side, but there is only air. Finally, he rises.

First he sees a waterfall cascading down to the side of him. Above him the ceiling climbs up at least twenty feet into overhead space. When he turns away from the waterfall, the cave stretches at least twenty feet ahead of him. He can hardly believe the size of this passage. He peels back his mask and lets it ride on his forehead and peers into the dark space, flashing his scout light back and forth. The water is pounding beside him. He screams. He feels ecstatic. Clearly this is a huge find. He screams again. The cavern is spacious, and his voice trails away in an echo. An echo! Its reverberation suggests the passage is larger than what he can see from down here and that it reaches into untold distance.

This makes him whoop again. And then he remembers his finger spool. He'll tell the others. But it is hard to contain such enthusiasm. He barely counts. He yanks and yanks and yanks--staccato, so there will be no question it is a signal.

Forty-five feet away, in the narrow space in front of the entry sump, the cavers' lights cast shadows in the darkness. To pass the time, Ackerman, who over his career has probably opened up many miles of wild cave, shares some of his exploits. It is cold and wet, and they have begun to cool down after the long haul and effort it took to get here.

Last time, on Preston's second effort to move through this sump, there was a moment when the others feared something happened to him. They were staring into the muddy sump water, watching his bubbles rise to the surface, comforted by the steady *blub-blub-blub*. And then he swam into the tight vertical, dead-end passage. At that point his air rose into the vertical cavity and stopped. Back at the sump, his bubbles ceased to roil the muddy surface. The pool grew still, and the others grew quiet in the dark.

They waited.

Nothing.

"Please," Ackerman intoned to himself. "Let him be safe."

And then they felt a tug on Preston's dive reel line. He was safe and still moving, but there was no doubt about the tug. He had not found a new cave passage.

On this attempt, when the surface stops bubbling, they all murmur in collective hope for Preston's safety. They remember the last time. This time, the bubbles seem to stop for quite a while. Dave Owen, holding the other end of Preston's finger spool, still feels movement on the line, like a huge sturgeon nibbling some deep-set bait.

"He's still moving around down there," Owen informs the others.

Ackerman continues passing the time telling them another cave story. And then Owen suddenly says, "Shuh!"

He has felt something. One solid jerk. "He's telling us something."

The others pause, only a second, and their collective lights shine on the line. They see another jerk. And another. Then another.

"How many?" Ackerman asks.

"Four," Owen says.

They watch the line pull again, and again, as though it is a deep-sea fishing line and Owen has hooked something very, very big.

"Five," he adds. "Six, seven, eight, nine, ten!" Owen says, smiling. At first he's worried. After the pulls stop, he answers with a tug of his own. Another tug comes back to verify, and Owen suspects he knows what it means. It means Preston has discovered something big. Something very big.

Owen grins. "He's found it!"

There is elation in his voice. The others whoop in the narrow space, their hollers fading behind them in the echoing Side Tributary passage.

Ackerman marks the time. Preston has one hour to explore what he has found and get back safe. Ackerman can't wait.

After sending his ecstatic message, Preston looks for a jagged edge of rock to tie off his dive reel. It has to be secure so he can anchor it and know it will hold. After searching for a while along the walls, he finally selects a protuberance near the falling water and ties off the reel, testing it to make certain it is securely fastened. Good. Nothing is certain in this kind of environment, but he thinks it will hold.

Now he has to get out and up these narrow walls. It doesn't look easy. He is careful with his equipment. He affixes his mask over his regulator and one side tank in a way that will keep them all safe. He can just reach up to a ledge near the edge of the waterfall, and he carefully tucks the tank, regulator, and mask up onto it. He swings up his other tank, makes sure its air is clearly turned off, and adds it to the rest of his equipment on the ledge. For a second he thinks about taking off his ten-pound weight belt but then decides he had better not. He is already tired. If he accidentally dropped the weight belt and it plummeted to the bottom, it would take too much effort and air to submerge himself and search blind along the raw, rock-strewn floor.

The opening is narrow, and Preston can chimney-crawl the five vertical feet required to climb to level ground. He places his legs across the narrow space and braces himself, using his gloved hands to support himself on the opposite wall, gradually scaling the tight passage. The climb is not easy, and the side walls, washed by eons of water flow and jagged edged from the ageless scour, cut into his dive suit. In fact, once he is up and out of the passage, blowing hard to recover his breath, he realizes it is very, very long and that it is entirely sharp edged and dangerous. He gathers his equipment and moves it twenty paces forward to a high, level, secure, dry spot. He double-checks his air to make certain both tanks are turned off. To have a slow leak in this passage, with his air bleeding out of a loose valve, would mean almost certain death. There is no backup. He has come into this space entirely alone, with no plans for what might happen if he cannot return.

The tanks are turned down tight, with plenty of air left and no leaks.

Finally, he takes a look at what lies in front of him.

There are two ways forward. Behind him, away from his watery entrance, the cave appears to widen. To the right, a pile of breakdown would require scaling about ten feet. To the left, where the shallow water of the stream runs, there is a flat, pebbly path about three to four feet high that would require some crawling. But it looks open up ahead, and he decides to venture into the watery entrance, knowing it will make a well-marked trail the deeper he enters the cave. He doesn't have to crawl very far before the cave opens up and he is standing, slightly bent, in a vertical space over five feet. He looks ahead, and the passage forks again. To the right, there is a continuance of the passage with the breakdown. It looks spacious and dry and appears to open up. To the left is a narrower passage with more water, but it also appears to open up. This time, Preston moves to the right toward a dome-shaped passage. This passage has a dry floor and smooth walls and opens up quickly. The ceiling rises to twenty feet. It is a dramatic underground cavernous space. He turns back into the watery passage and shines his light. He sees that it appears to run on for another spacious one hundred feet into more cave. He enters the space and after another seventy-five feet of careful walking, to avoid stepping into a watery gouge and twisting or breaking an ankle, he encounters a passage with beautiful flowstone, some curtain formations, and similar geologic structure.

He carries a portable camera in two sealed plastic bags, and he tries to take photos. But the camera is cheap, and in his excitement he has already dropped it into the water several times. The small lens fogs up in the cold cave air. He licks the lens and photographs the flowstone. Luckily, the flash still fires. Then he re-stows the camera and peers ahead.

Preston's hands are trembling. The combination of exertion and excitement is taking its toll. This cave is big. It appears to run on forever. He walks another fifty feet down this passage and encounters another Y. Off to the right is more dry, spacious cave. Off to the left, the watery way continues, also spacious and open as far as he can see.

He checks his watch. His sump exit crawl and careful movement through the cave has taken up thirty minutes. Time to turn back.

* * *

At the level place in front of the cave passage, he readies his equipment. He retightens his harness and stows his camera in the double-sealed bags in the bellows bag attached to his side. He checks the regulator, and the airflow is good. Getting back into the narrow sump is a trick. He brings the equipment down to the nearby ledge and settles it there, then shimmies down into the still-turbid water. Once in the water, he drags his tanks down and attaches them to his harness, checks his regulator and mask, and feels ready. He peers into the water, holding his scout light right in front, but it is dark as pitch. He can't see anything. He looks up and double-checks the anchored dive line, just to make sure it is tight. And then he takes careful hold of the narrow white line—his lifeline—and he drops into the cloudy dark.

He cannot remember much about his passage out. He follows the line and doesn't think, and it is one of the easiest blind traverses along a tactile line he has ever made. When he feels the final turn and starts to rise, he can feel the pressure in his ears equalizing.

On the other side, seven cold companions await his return. They have been sharing more stories about the cave, trying to not worry, to stay focused and warm.

When Dave Owen feels the line movement, he lets the others know Preston is on his way back. After several tense moments, they watch some bubbles rise to the turbid surface. Preston comes in just behind them. He takes off his mask and lets out a whoop and proceeds to talk nonstop about what he found on the other side. Eventually he gets out of the pool. But Preston doesn't stop talking. He is like a Super Bowl quarterback who has just won the game, jabbering on and on without pause. He tells them about the dive and the sump and the waterfall and the dry passage and the flowstone and how the cave on the other side goes on forever, farther than he could go in just one half hour.

Finally, after Owen and the others have helped him off with his gear, excited by his remarkable news, they start back toward David's Entrance and the long climb to the surface.

Ackerman has been asking questions about the cave on the other side. He has been asking about the dive, too. As they near the ladder, he grows silent. The others move and talk behind him. They wait by the entrance, taking their turns ascending the steel ladder.

Finally, Ackerman sidles up beside Preston and whispers words he knows he will regret. But he cannot help himself. The mystery of what lies on the other side of that sump compels him.

"I'm going in," he says.

The last thing John Ackerman wants to do is dive another cave sump. But he and John Preston have worked throughout the last month preparing for this moment, reviewing the entire trip more times than he can count. They have carefully compiled just the right mixture of scuba gear, surveying equipment, and survival provisions. And here he is, suiting up with Preston to scuba dive a tight, difficult crossing into the newly discovered cave—now named the Iconoclast Section.

Ackerman has spent hours—and, most recently, sleepless nights—contemplating every detail of this dive. He has worried over every inch of Preston's pencil-drawn sketch. The angled rocky descent of almost twenty feet that stops at a rock wall. The right turn into a harrowing tunnel with a flat, sandy bottom. The few more feet of straight passage that turns into a vertical chute, rising twelve feet and surfacing under a thundering waterfall.

He can trace that passage on a paper napkin. What he wonders now is why he ever agreed to come.

Once again, they gear up in the narrow passage twenty feet back from the lip of the entry point, so the water will remain clear. Clay Kraus, Dave Gerboth, and Charlie Graling, who have helped carry loads for this trip, listen to the two discuss, try to help. But the divers are in some other zone, a region permeated with fear, driven by adrenaline, riddled with a rising pitch of excitement that is palpable in the dark underworld passage.

Preston can feel Ackerman's anxiety. It is completely understandable, even warranted. They have already spent so much time planning and talking about this excursion, this misadventure, this great exploration and survey, there is no other reason for rehashing the trip except to blow off steam.

"We just follow the cave line," Preston says. He hopes the line is still well anchored and taut. The thin nylon cord has been stretched almost forty-five feet through the underwater passage for nearly a month. "And then there's the silt," Preston adds. "I wish the current were stronger. As soon as we enter

the water, this place will turn dark as a coal digger's backside."
Preston doesn't smile when saying that.

Although the dive is dangerous, maybe even foolhardy,
perhaps downright crazy, Ackerman must see with his own
eyes what lies on the other side. His desire to explore pristine
cave exceeds his fear. But only by the thinnest margin.

Getting to the sump has already felt like a day's work. This
time, they hauled enough gear for two divers as well as everything required to explore and survey a large, pristine cave of
unknown length. And this time, they are allowing themselves
plenty of time for the exploration, approximately eight hours.

Walking on the surface, in a straight line, the 850-foot trek
would be easy—just shy of a football field. But down here it is
completely dark, and they are twisting and turning through a
catacomb with wild walls and jagged edges and a rock-strewn,
watery floor.

The seventy-five feet of passage from the bottom of David's
Entrance to the Side Tributary is the easy part. Kraus, Gerboth, Graling, and the two Johns ferry the equipment to the
entry point. After a brief pause, they start into the longer
length of water-filled side channel. They wade through knee-
deep water, sometimes squatting to move through its sharp-
edged length. In the twists and turns, there are places where
they have to wedge through sideways, arms extended and bur-
dened with dive tanks, back plates, and related gear. Their del-
toids strain with the effort. It is back-breaking labor.

But now it's done.

When they gathered their gear on top, it was 10:00 AM and
18 degrees. By the time they haul their gear down the cavern
length, holding at its steady 47 degrees, and suit up at the entryway, it is 11:40 AM, and they are warmed by the exertion.

* * *

But right now Ackerman isn't thinking about being over-heated. He is not thinking about their return from the other side. Right now he is only thinking about making it from this side to the next.

Digital camera, ten AAA batteries, emergency blanket, candle and waterproof matches, mini-tripod, four glow sticks, eye drops, Band-Aids, and Advil, all stuffed into one watertight canister for dry transport to the other side.

Camera flash, second emergency blanket, backup head-lamp, multipurpose knife/tool, line markers, cleaning cloth, and extra ziplock bags, in another canister.

Preston carries a wet notes board for taking notes in inclement environs, with a clip, two mini backup lights, a main headlamp, more batteries, two bottles of water, four Power Bars, and a small spool.

This is the lightest portion of their equipment. Ackerman wears a stainless-steel back plate with a side harness for holding a forty-cubic-foot air tank on the left. He wears a fifteen-pound weight belt—and, of course, he carefully secures a line-cutting tool in his waistband. He has a scout light with a small pack on his right side and another light attached with a lanyard to his wrist.

Preston has been wearing his fourteen-pound weight belt since he descended the ladder from up top. Now he affixes his harness and attaches the forty-cubic-foot tank to it, tucked under his left arm, at his side. He, too, slips a standard line-cutting tool into his belt. Then he attaches one of their supply canisters to his right side and the second canister to his left, tucked up beside his tank. He has his Halcyon bellows pocket attached to his left side. The bellows pocket holds his wet notes, two bottles of water, a fifty-foot tape measure, and his headlamp. On a right-side waist ring he has hooked a second safety spool. And on his left-side ring he has attached a compass. He sticks his cave gloves and some related gear into the back of his wet suit and wears his dive timer and a scout light on his left hand.

"Okay," he says to Ackerman. "Let's roll."

Ackerman checks his regulator, and the airflow is good. He checks his mask and clears it one last time.

"If we aren't back by 8:00 PM, you know what to do," he calls back to Gerboth, Kraus, and Graling.

"We know," they say almost in unison.

They hope they never have to act on the plan. If the divers don't return, another cave diver on standby can reach the site within an hour and will try to follow them in. Ackerman has also brought along a small radio transmitter. If they become hurt or for some other reason cannot exit the cave and return, he'll set up the transmitter in the best location he can find. A drilling rig is also on call. Drilling would take time, but if they knew where to dig, they'd make it down.

Ackerman crosses the twenty feet of stream length toward the sump. He is careful to move so his steps won't rile the water and start clouding the narrow pool. He glances over the edge and peers into the lucid waters.

He can see the white dive line Preston laid down on his earlier dive disappearing into the long, rocky corridor. And now Ackerman is going to enter the Side Tributary sump while the water is clear. And he will stay just ahead of the silt-out.

Preston will follow him blind.

Ackerman enters the shallow end of the sump and begins to lower himself into the clear water. He has carefully positioned his gear so he will avoid another line entanglement like the one that almost took his life. The water is cold, and he tries to concentrate on the tactile sense of it. Mentally, emotionally, he is wound up tight as a choked dive reel, and he knows he has to stop thinking about it. He tries to take one long breath and blow out his anxiety with his exhale. But it isn't working.

The edges of the sump behind him are already starting to cloud. He tries to lower himself deeper into the clear end of the pool, but he feels too buoyant. The extra pound he has given himself on his weight belt isn't enough. He tries to bob and turn and get down under the surface. The water starts to cloud behind and around him, and he knows if he wants to get through this passage he is going to have to get down before the water is completely riled and silted in. He will not enter that passage blind, and so he turns and grabs hold of the jagged-edged side and pulls himself down. The effort riles more water behind and around him, but when he peers down, he can still see the clear, boulder-strewn corridor length angling down away from the sump's entrance, disappearing into darkness. He turns and kicks, and suddenly he is under the surface.

His light shines along the white dive line as he dives deeper. But when he looks up ahead, just another four or five feet down the angled slope, what he sees shocks him. The line disappears beneath four or five large limestone slabs.

Ackerman stops. He shines his light along the corridor's roof, but even in the shadows it looks solid and clean. It must be breakdown from Preston's last fractious exit. Carefully, his heart pumping in his ears, remembering to breathe, the sound of his exhaling bubbles rising into the sump behind him, he moves along the line. He ventures to the point where it disappears beneath the limestone slabs, and he spends a few precious seconds pulling the rocks off of the line. He watches them tumble down the corridor slope, trailing smoke behind them. Now the white dive line is free, but the water is clouding in. Unless he moves quickly, he will have to resurface and call off the dive.

He pushes down the length and gets beyond the clouded water, and his clarity returns. He comes to the blank wall Preston described to him earlier and sketched in crude pencil, and he instinctively turns right. And suddenly he is in a long, low, flat, sandy passage, and for just one instant it appears inviting, and he pushes farther into the passage along the clear bottom.

But what he feels next threatens to undo him. He feels the safety line drag along over his hoses, along his harness, down his right leg. He feels himself becoming entangled. He has a fleeting moment of panic. He wants to scurry ahead, leap toward the surface he imagines must be close. Or turn around. But behind him the silty water is following like a reaching dark cloud. If he moves suddenly ahead, he is likely to become more entangled.

He inches forward slowly. He remembers the dragon. The one inside his head that threatened his life just four years ago. The one he has to face down. He cannot panic. He was able to survive his first cave dive by remaining calm.

But his heart feels trapped in its narrow bone cage, and his head is screaming run, swim, surface, and it is all Ackerman can do to inch slowly forward and struggle to remain calm. Ackerman's progress has been slow. Behind him, Preston waited a full two minutes before entering the sump. By the time he lowered himself into the water, it was almost entirely clouded over. He looked down, gathered the line in his right hand, made sure he could feel it and sense its angled trajectory into the boulder-strewn corridor, and dropped headfirst into the abyss.

For all his experience underwater in tight situations, Preston doesn't like the silted-out, sharp-edged quarters typical of diving Minnesota's karst region. He carefully descends into the corridor. He can see the water riled in front of him. Near the bottom he levels out and senses the moment when he is about to hit the wall.

His hand feels the structure, and he gropes in the darkness to be certain it is the wall. And then he turns right, moving along what he knows is the sandy bottom. He is still holding the line, still moving along its almost invisible length.

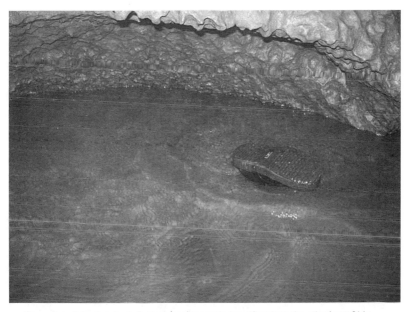

Cave diver John Preston's foot as he descends headfirst into the silted-out Side Tributary sump. Courtesy John Ackerman

And then suddenly there is a foot in front of him. He can see it only inches away, with the white dive line wrapped around it. Even through the murky darkness, he can almost feel the foot's tension.

Preston reaches forward and gives the line a simple, freeing twist, and the rope drops away. The foot flashes as it disappears in the murk. Preston waits.

Ackerman can still see in front of him. He has not felt Preston's hand move down the line and slip it from his foot. But he senses some kind of release, and, unencumbered, he kicks forward.

He hears something. He looks up, and his light shines through ten feet of clear, narrow passage. What he sees sends

Exiting the sump in the Iconoclast Section, Goliath's Cave. Courtesy John Preston

an electric jolt through his entire frame. He rises to the sound of pounding water, to the image of clear water falling on the surface of a pool in a cave he has never seen.

When he rises into the narrow sump with the five-foot waterfall drumming its surface, he sees exactly what Preston told him. The walls rise in a pockmarked, vertical climb at least five feet before he can exit and get out of his gear. Ackerman chimneys up the narrow space quickly and efficiently, stepping off to the side and shedding almost all of his gear before Preston's head breaks the cloudy surface.

Preston is bigger than Ackerman and not as adept at climbing out of tight quarters. He struggles with his burden. Ackerman reaches down and gives him a hand with his gear, and then a hand up.

In the close confines of this chamber, the waterfall thunders and the men can barely hear each other's whoops. They recognize each other's smiles. Preston motions to the place where he stowed his gear the only other time anyone has been here. Ackerman picks up his equipment and starts walking down the narrow cave.

He is impressed with this entrance, much larger than what he expected. And the dry, spacious sit-down room is the perfect place to stow their gear and get their bearings. Ackerman's heart is still singing a few octaves higher than its normal pitch. The second he broke the surface of the pool, he felt he had again cheated death. His adrenaline has not yet ebbed. The realization that eventually he will have to climb back into that underwater maze, and this time more than likely without visibility, is so far in the back of his mind it is barely a thought.

19
Exploration, Survey, and Return
Goliath's Cave, the Iconoclast Section
Saturday, November 26, 2005

Right now, staring ahead into a passage that seems to run straight and clear into the dark, with no end in sight, John Ackerman feels like a boy again. That feeling the first time he sees something so beautiful and unexpected and rare his heart pauses in its beat and his breath stops, because it feels like he has just been broken open like an egg.

Twenty-five paces beyond the thundering waterfall, he and John Preston can finally hear each other speak.

"Can you pull that out of my back?" Preston asks, turning around.

Tucked into the rear of his wet suit, Preston has a pair of caving gloves and his LED headlamp. Ackerman is impressed with his foresight. He hands Preston the articles and takes a moment to affix his own LED headlamp. He keeps panning around this passage and the narrow opening ahead. It is low and sharp edged. He recognizes Stewartville rock formation. Over the millennia, the constant water scour has created a low-ceilinged limestone corridor with tiny quill-like spines sticking out of the walls.

"Looks like trouble for the new wet suits," Ackerman says, grinning.

Preston stares into the shadowy corridor. "We're going to get holes," he says. The last time he came into this passage, the walls made several small tears in his wet suit. "It starts to open up ahead," he nods.

After a brief discussion about how best to begin, Ackerman agrees to take the lead. He will carry one end of the fifty-foot survey tape up into the cave passage. If he does not find a side passage or a branch or sharp turn, he will crawl to the end of fifty feet. If he finds a turn in the corridor or some other interesting feature, he will stop.

He can see the passage narrow up ahead, though it continues straight and true. He squats down and starts to duckwalk into the shallow stream, finally leaning over into a hand-and-foot crawl, searching for the right holds along the pebbly bottom. He travels twenty-three feet before the ceiling starts to rise. He stops and lets Preston bring up the survey tape slack.

The simplest place to store the unraveled tape is around his left arm. As Preston approaches, Ackerman winds the tape round and round his wrist. They are both crouched into this four-foot-high, sharp-edged corridor. Preston pulls out his wet notes and records the measurement and a compass reading. Then he smiles.

"Pretty incredible, huh?"

They can both see the passage open up ahead, with the ceiling starting to rise.

John Preston in the low-lying area near the Iconoclast entry sump. The initial crawl into the Iconoclast section lies ahead. Courtesy John Preston

"Amazing," Ackerman agrees. "Incredible." And then he is off, his enthusiasm as palpable as their echoes.

Preston knows only part of what rises in front of them. Now that he is here with an experienced caver, he can pause to appreciate the find. Judging from Ackerman's initial superlatives—"Wow!" "Extraordinary!" "Unbelievable!"— Preston guesses it is as special as he suspected. As Ackerman rubbernecks into the corridor, peering at all sides of the new passage, the superlatives diminish until he is finally dumb-struck by the cave's beauty.

They now have one thing Preston didn't when he was here before: time. Preston had fewer than thirty minutes. This time they arrive in the cave around noon. Their partners waiting on the other side expect them back at or before 8:00 PM. Eight hours should be plenty of time, providing they don't break an ankle, leg, or neck—or worse, run out of battery power.

Up ahead the way is narrow, and they have to move for-ward in a crawl across a hard pebbled floor through the clear stream. Soon the walking becomes easier.

Preston knows Ackerman will want to push leads, explore possible new sections, probe dark crevices. For the moment he is comforted by the fact the corridor becomes easier the far-ther they move into it.

Ackerman steps off another seventeen feet, letting out sur-vey tape as he duckwalks through the passage. At a Y branch, the stream flows toward them down the left channel. Up ahead, the branch they are in goes straight and dry for around twenty feet. The ceiling rises, and Ackerman can see break-down spread across the cave floor with what he thinks is the dark start of a passage to the right and left.

Preston approaches and makes another notation on his wet

notes board. They are happy to be crawling into rising passage. By the time they measure off twenty-four feet straight into the watery left branch, and over thirty feet straight ahead into the side branch, with another passage turning to the right and its extension continuing left where it picks up the streambed passage, they have surveyed another sixty feet. More importantly, they are standing in the cave with lots of ceiling room. And the ceiling appears to be rising.

They continue the same process for the next two hours, Ackerman taking the measure ahead and anchoring its end (if he unrolls the entire fifty feet) to some kind of rocky protuberance, of which there are many. It is so easy to find places to anchor the survey tape's steel ring Ackerman says, "This cave must want to be measured!"

They laugh in the dark.

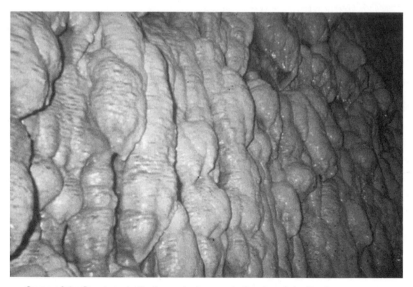

Some of the flowstone in the Iconoclast passage. Courtesy John Preston

Preston picks up the survey tape slack and walks ahead to meet him, then takes a compass reading and jots the length and reading on his board.

Near the end of the first two to three hundred feet, they find a massive flowstone coming down the left wall. As the ceiling gets higher, Ackerman sees eighteen-inch soda straws.

"Those are some of the longest soda straws I've ever seen," he comments.

"I told you it was something," Preston exhales into the darkness.

"You were damn right about that," Ackerman says.

They are so busy measuring and rubbernecking and examining, they don't have much time for talking. At first, Ackerman wants to test every small side passage or dark crevasse, exploring as far as they can. More than a third of the way into the system, Ackerman insists on pushing a progressively narrowing section of cave. This section is wet, and by the time they are down to a side worm crawl, Preston has had enough.

"I'm turning around," Preston says. He can see Ackerman's feet ahead of him.

"Okay," Ackerman answers. "I'm just going to push it a little farther."

Preston is more comfortable pushing tight underwater passages in full scuba gear and blackout conditions than he is pushing these narrowing leads through cold, black, smelly mud. He manages to turn around and crawl back to the main passage.

Ackerman hopes he is entering a passage that will open into another easy walking section with more cave stretching out ahead of him. But after twenty more feet, his progress is halted at the bottom of what he suspects is a sinkhole.

They mark off the length of passage and backtrack to the streambed. They are both covered in mud. The air is redolent with the smell of decomposition, of river bottom. Preston is happy to be back in the stream, where they wash off and continue surveying the main corridor.

Ackerman is simply stunned. At one point he rounds a corner into a passage with a thirty-foot-high ceiling dramatically stretching above them and, shaking his head, says, "It would be incredible if we surveyed over a thousand feet of new cave. This place is a wonderland."

Preston is behind him, taking up the rear and making his latest annotation. He looks down and, under the light of his headlamp, makes some quick calculations. Then he laughs. "We're already at over nine hundred feet!" he exclaims.

They look up ahead to a wide, tall passage that runs on into darkness. Preston looks at his grinning companion, and their combined laughter echoes away through the high cavern walls.

Farther down, they find dry upper-level passages. As they continue along the stream, they find more side passages. Some have water flowing through them. Others are dry.

After almost four hours of pushing leads and measuring cave length, they know they are running low on time. By now they have rough-surveyed well over a thousand feet of new cave, with incredible formations and geologic structures and side entries that disappear into darkness filled with the potential for miles of more cave. They are stunned but know they must soon turn back. Finally, thankfully, they reach the end of this major passage and cannot proceed any farther. They have logged 1,542 feet.

The time is 4:40. They have to be out by 8:00. They must turn around and find their way back to the Iconoclast sump and their gear. In all their zigzag, herky-jerky movement through the cave, bypassing side channels and forks in the main channel, they have always tried to keep to the watery course, so they will be able to follow the stream to the sump. If they stick to the streambed and watch for key landmarks—a rusted can embedded in the cave wall, the white flowstone, and similar physical markers—they know they'll be able to retrace their steps. And Preston has his survey notes and compass readings, just in case.

But first they have to make it back to their cache of batteries. Almost two hours earlier, they set down the small pack with backup batteries at a nondescript intersection, hoping to simplify their move and measure down virgin passage. But they had not anticipated continuing to survey for two more hours. Now there is a real possibility that their headlamps could run out of power and plunge them into absolute darkness. They are both determined to make it back to their cache as quickly as possible. To walk blind through this much sharp-edged cave could be deadly.

But Preston is pretty sure he knows the way. By his compass they have moved in a westerly direction, with a slight southern slant to it. Ackerman lets him lead.

After over an hour of steady slogging through the main corridor, both of them begin to fear they have taken some sort of wrong turn. They have entered a section of unfamiliar cave, and Preston is having trouble getting his bearings.

"Just a minute," he says. "I need to check my notes."

Ackerman waits while Preston examines his wet board. He looks from his notes up to the corridor ahead. There is a branch, and when he gazes down the branch he sees what looks like familiar breakdown.

"The nice thing about being lost," Ackerman says, "is I won't have to make that dive back to the other side."

Preston does not laugh, because right now he is a little worried. He is focusing on his notes. "Let's check this out," he says.

They move forward to the breakdown, and Preston sees an aerosol can, washed down from some surface dump, wedged into the wall. He remembers it from their earlier passage. But behind them the watery course moves down another passage. Then he realizes they have stumbled on a shortcut that will lead them back to the main passage and their cache. When he tests his theory by walking into the watery passage, he sees signs of their passing. Preston is relieved.

But Ackerman is continuing to worry about that dive. They are leaving this place of astonishing beauty. And they are going into an underwater passage that they may be able to navigate only by blind feel, with rocky protrusions and dead ends and places where a gloved hand can easily become separated from a narrow white dive line.

"Do you think the water will be clear?" Ackerman asks.

"Nope," Preston answers. "I very much doubt it's going to be clear." He knows the sump will be silted in. They haven't been gone long enough for the water to clear or the mud to settle.

"Maybe it will be a little clear," Ackerman says hopefully.

Preston wants him to begin preparing for the trip into underwater darkness. "Maybe," he says, "but I suspect we'll have zero vis," he repeats.

"We've been gone over five hours," Ackerman argues.

"The water doesn't look to me like it's been moving fast enough. And we've been clouding up this little stream as we've been walking. It dumps into that sump," he reasons.

They come to the intersection with their cache and are thankful to have the backup batteries. They continue, but the closer they come to the exit sump, the more comments and questions Ackerman has about the dive. A few hours ago, when he broke the surface of the new cave, he thought he had again cheated death, and he may have been right. In cave diving, healthy respect can easily bleed into fear. It is the kind of anxiety that feeds the irrational mind. He can't keep himself from asking obvious questions, the ones whose answers he already understands so well.

The questions and answers continue, all the way to the exit sump.

As they sit down and drink some water, devouring a couple of Power Bars, they marvel over the passage they've just surveyed. They are still amazed. The water and chocolate peanut butter bar taste good and for a moment divert Ackerman's fear into something more pleasurable, satisfying, and tactile. But only for a moment.

"I hope I make it back alive," he says.

Preston laughs, but there isn't a lot of humor in the comment.

It takes a while to gear up. Probably longer than normal, because Ackerman keeps asking *what-ifs*. Preston patiently answers each of them. He helps Ackerman with his gear, carefully affixing the harness so his side tank rides easily beside him. Ackerman carefully positions his line cutter in the sheath along his left side. It saved his life once. It might have to again.

After both of them are suited up and ready, they proceed to the sump and the thundering waterfall. Sure enough, the white dive line disappears only an inch or two under the cloudy surface. The water is an opaque brown, completely silted in.

Ackerman delays, asking a couple of other questions. Preston patiently answers him but reminds him they should be getting back. Finally, Ackerman uses his back and knees to chimney-crawl down the narrow space, hovering just above the surface. He stares at the narrow white line.

"The line is your friend," Preston reminds him.

"Yeah, right," Ackerman responds. It wasn't his friend the last time he dove into blackout conditions.

"Don't let go of it," Preston counsels. "Keep it to your left and slide it through your hand as you inch forward. It will take you all the way out."

"Easier said than done," he replies, staring at the line. "What if it works its way into a crack, or there's some new breakdown covering it?"

"Do exactly what I said before. Keep your body away from the line and hold it at arm's length. Your body will feel its way through the largest portion of the passage and you will have no trouble," Preston shouts.

"Wonderful. Now I know where I got it wrong before. I was thinking too much!"

Preston is nodding. "That's right," he answers. "Don't think. Just close your eyes, concentrate on the line, and feel yourself across. You won't even need your light."

Ackerman stares up at his companion. "There is no way I'm going into that death trap without my light on," he says. Preston knows it will be virtually useless down below. "Hold it two inches away from the line and follow it," he relents.

Ackerman knows he is buying time. It is like being at the top of a cliff before jumping into water you think is safe, but you aren't sure. It doesn't make the jump any easier. But at some point you realize that thinking about your body's rapid drop through the air, the smack on the water, is actually making the jump harder.

So finally Ackerman nods, puts his regulator into his mouth, takes two test breaths, and drops feetfirst into the narrow sump.

He is careful with the line. He holds it in his left hand and follows it twelve feet to the bottom. He can feel the pressure in his ears. He moves his jaw and swallows and equalizes his inner ear. The descent is tight. He touches the sides as he drops. The only sound is the Darth Vader inhale and his bubbly exhale. His light is on, but he cannot see more than six to eight inches in the murk. His light is connected to his hand with a lanyard, and occasionally he catches a dull glow in the murky depth.

When he feels the bottom, he is relieved. He takes a moment to try his light. He is actually able to shine it a few inches from a rocky protuberance. He knows he will have to bend down, and now he reaches for that narrow opening at the bottom that leads to the flat wall and the left turn up the corridor. He can see the entire passage in his head. He finds the tunnel by feel and begins dropping feetfirst into it, still careful to keep the line at his side, avoiding that protruding rock. And just when his anxiety begins to diminish and he starts to feel something more positive about his flawless descent and continued passage to the other side—something he now thinks he might be able to manage—he feels a tug at his side. He pulls, just a little, but he can feel the pull behind him. With his free right hand, he feels around to his side and suddenly realizes his tank is behind him. His harness has become loose and floated up behind him and gotten wedged in the bottom of the chute.

Damn! Now what? Ackerman can recognize when the pitch of his heart rate ratchets up a notch. It's happening now. Try to work around in these tight quarters and stow the tank in the harness blind? Or resurface? It doesn't take him long to decide. He backs up the shoot, keeping the tank near him, and resurfaces in the Iconoclast sump just as Preston is getting ready to follow him in.

Preston is surprised when Ackerman surfaces. Perhaps more like stunned and then worried.

He waits for Ackerman's regulator to come off.

"I've come back to the party," Ackerman shouts, trying to be light about it.

Preston is not amused. These tanks should have plenty of air. And if you follow the rope it shouldn't take more than a few minutes to make the crossing. They probably didn't use much air on the way over. But he knows there is a limit to their oxygen, and he hopes there is a good reason for Ackerman resurfacing.

Ackerman senses his dismay. "My harness is coming off," he explains.

Preston backs out of the sump and removes his tank. Ackerman follows him out so Preston can readjust the harness.

Once the harness is fixed, Preston turns to him and says, "Good to go," while the waterfall pounds the surface behind them.

Ackerman puts the regulator back into his mouth, takes two tentative breaths, and gives Preston the thumbs-up. But he is not thinking *thumbs-up*. He is thinking how unfortunate he is to have to do this descent a second time.

This time he gets it right. This time he moves slowly down the line, equalizes pressure in his ears as he drops down the twelve-foot chute and finds the bottom with his feet. He also feels for the opening. If he holds the light two to three inches from the line, he can see it. And he can barely feel it as it moves through his left hand. He drops into the passage with the sand bottom and makes his way to the wall. He finds it, turns left, and begins his gradual angled ascent up through the boulder-strewn corridor.

And now he is feeling good about it. Just as he gets close to the surface, he sees lights. It is Kraus's million-candle-watt headlamp, and he can see it near the surface, and he rises to the light. Like coming back to life, he thinks.

He breaks the surface, takes the regulator out of his mouth, and exclaims, "it's good to be alive!"

The others are happy to see him.

Back down in the murky depths, Preston has followed Ackerman. He gives the caver some time to find his way well into the passage, not wanting to drop on top of him or meet up with him underground. As he drops into the sump and begins to descend, he notices his air grow a little tight. His regulator is becoming stingy with its release of oxygen. He wonders about it.

Then he reaches the bottom of the narrow chute, and suddenly his air is off.

Most people would resurface, but Preston is a seasoned diver. He sits in the murky depth, unable to take a breath, and thinks about it. He knows he has more than enough air to make this crossing. Probably enough to make it ten times! He is the pack mule on this trip. He has a canister on his left side with his tank, one on his right. And he is a big guy. On the way down he was bumping along the side. And then he thinks he knows what's wrong.

He reaches up behind him and along his tank until he feels the top valve. He gives it a quick turn. The air flows back into his regulator, and he breathes. He takes another breath and gives the valve another twist.

On the way down, his tank valve knocked against the rocky side of the descent chute, and after a couple of well-placed bumps, his air valve was shut off.

When he tells the story up top, after arising into the Side Tributary sump passage, Ackerman is amazed. "I would have shot up to the surface in a second," he says.

The two divers are exhausted. It has been a very, very long day. They drag their equipment out of the Side Tributary passage, out into the main passage to David's Entrance. They still need to haul it all up the seventy-five-foot chute and climb the ladder, and they are truly, truly tired. But as the others help them out with their gear, neither of them can stop talking about their find. In that underground darkness, tromping through the shallow stream down beautiful cave passages, something remarkable has happened. They have surveyed and added 1,582 feet to Goliath's, exactly what Ackerman expected would happen when he opened this cave for further exploration. He feels vindicated about all his hard work, expense, and risk. He feels very, very good.

As Preston counts the tears in his wet suit—there are thirty-one—he asks Ackerman when he wants to go back. But Ackerman isn't interested in tempting fate a third time. Besides, he has a pretty good idea that the end of that westerly passage could be very close to the surface, or a nearby sinkhole. Ackerman and his caving companions Dave Gerboth and Clay Kraus are already thinking about how they might be able to sink a dry entrance into this remarkable new section. But of course there are political concerns. Ackerman is fairly certain this new passage wanders under DNR/SNA land. If a potential dry entrance fell within the boundaries of Cherry Grove, they would never be able to create it. They will just have to see. For now the veteran caver is pleased.

Preston would return twice more, once for a photo shoot, again for a radio location of the farthest part of the cave. Both dives would be solo.

20

Beyond the Rubicon
At David's Entrance and the farthest reaches
  of Goliath's Cave
Saturday, October 11, 2008

John Ackerman and Clay Kraus gather their thirty-foot cable
ladder, rock drill, bolt, hanger, and related equipment and
lower it down the seventy-five-foot drop to the passage below.
It will be a long day.

Ackerman enters first, climbing down David's Entrance, his hands and feet carefully gripping the steel ladder. Today he feels certain they are going to push beyond the farthest reaches of Goliath's Cave and find the elusive doorway that opens into an entirely new section of wandering, underground passages. He has come close twice in the recent past. Both times he came up to sections of cave that appeared to continue, but in each instance he was unable to proceed because he did not have the proper equipment—a wet suit or a drop rope or a ladder with something to bolt and anchor it. But today he has a fresh plan, a new way to reach the farthest point. Today he is going to traverse the entire length of the Rubicon and climb beyond its deep-set, dramatic waterfall, using higher, dry passages they have only recently discovered. Today he and Kraus wear dry caving clothes. And for that they are profoundly thankful.

Ackerman has been to this farthest point in Goliath's Cave only twice. It is not an easy place to reach. The last time, he wore his wet suit and undertook the dismal crawl through hundreds of feet of low-hanging streambed. It is an icy scrabble, but once your body heats the thin layer of water between the seven-mil wet suit and your skin, you can breathe again. Then all you have to worry about is the painful drag through rock and mud, with your neck arched to keep your mouth where you can continue gulping air.

And you *have* to keep your hard hat on. Scraping against the overhead rock's serrated surface is like grating the rind off an orange. And the only light source you have down here (apart from your two backups—Ackerman carries four), in the absolute center of cold darkness, is on top of your head.

During their last trip into these far reaches, Ackerman believes he and Kraus found a better way, sort of. This new path begins the usual way, with a descent through David's Entrance, then an east-southeast walk through the spacious streambed until you come to the east-northeast crawl-under that enters the Rubicon. This is the main southeasterly trending borehole through which Goliath's multiple streams converge and continue flowing east underground. It is not an easy hike. There are parts that require turning sideways to avoid cutting yourself on the cave's sharp-edged walls. Other places only require you to put out your gloved hand to steady yourself as you step along two opposing wall ledges perched five feet above a flowing stream.

Along the Rubicon, there are places where huge slabs of limestone have fallen from the ceiling and the relatively open passage is blocked. Then you have to carefully climb over the wreckage, or through it, if there is a big enough hole. All the while the ceiling keeps rising, first from ten to twelve feet, then quickly to twenty, then a hundred feet or more into the underground air. It is a deep-set cavern, truly amazing to see—even though your lights can barely penetrate into the far, curvy reaches of stone.

Ackerman and Kraus now traverse this passage, carrying the equipment that Ackerman feels certain will enable him to get farther than he has ever been. Ackerman's cave sense tells him they are very, very close to discovering a section of underground passage that will transform Goliath's Cave from just three miles of crisscrossed passages and dramatic rooms to possibly more than a dozen.

So for now the two cavers haul their equipment and themselves down the long, deep line of the Rubicon, reserving their strength for their final push.

* * *

Ackerman and Kraus have been down the Rubicon passage many times. But the way it begins to heighten and become more dramatic never ceases to amaze them. Ackerman can only guess what Magnusson, Madsen, and Lilja must have thought of it, coming as they had to from the cave's distant wild entrance. Those guys worked so hard to solve the entry problem—Lilja's brush with death, Magnusson's efforts to dig the second entrance—they had more right than most to be frustrated by the sna's closing of the cave.

Of course, many people both in the DNR and elsewhere believe the sna's acquisition and management of the cave is exactly what the cave needs. The sna's meticulous control of the site and restrictions on access into it will protect the cave for generations to come. DNR staff administer the sna properties as a trust for the people of Minnesota, and they are true to that trust.

On the other hand, Ackerman muses, as he and Kraus reach the midpoint of the Rubicon, given the sna's permit application rules and procedures, very few members of future generations will ever be able to *see* it. Ackerman appreciates the sna's mission. Part of the sna's stated goal addresses preserving Minnesota's ecological diversity "for scientific study and public edification." But if there is no way to enter the cave—if its entry is blocked, as it so often is—how can scientific study continue? And if no one can ever enter the cave, how will the public be edified?

The periodic blockage (man-made and natural) of the sna entrance is something Professor Calvin Alexander knows all too well. After Ackerman drilled his entrance into the lower portions of Goliath's Cave, there was an increase in the scientific permit applications filed and granted.

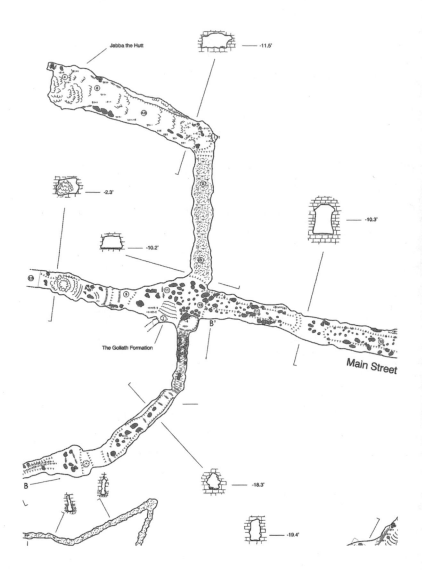

Detail of map of Goliath's Cave, Cherry Grove Blind Valley Scientific and Natural Area, by John Lovaas, data collected to December 2007. Courtesy Peggy Booth

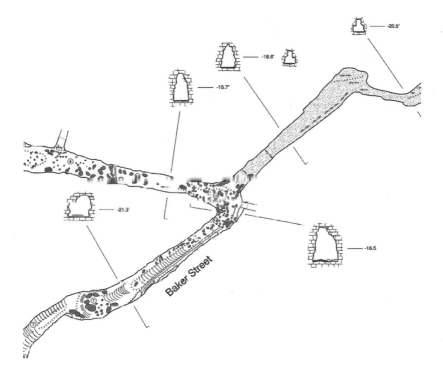

-20.5'

-18.6'

-15.7'

-21.3'

-18.5

Baker Street

On April 21, 2006, Dawn Ryan and John Lovaas were granted a permit to enter Goliath's Cave "for the purpose of conducting mapping and inventory of the cave system in the Cherry Grove Blind Valley SNA." The permit noted that Ryan and Lovaas "have a clear understanding of the purpose and long-term goal of State Scientific and Natural Areas."

As Alexander understood it, the natural cave entrance was blocked when Lovaas and Ryan started their survey, so they first had to clear away the debris and get the cave gate unlocked and opened. On November 19, 2006, Alexander actually assisted one of the crews mapping Goliath's Cave.

In February 2006, Alexander decided he would submit his own permit application. He recognized that after the drilling of David's Entrance there was more activity on the site. After a few questions back and forth to clarify aspects of his request, it was finally submitted April 11, 2007, and approved two days later. Alexander and DNR hydrologist Jeff Green would "document and study the hydrogeology of the Goliath Cave System."

By the time the SNA approved the professor's permit, the natural entrance was again choked with debris, rendering it impassable. Alexander offered to get together a group of university student volunteers to clean out the entrance. But the SNA declined his offer, citing liability concerns.

When the cave re-opened in the summer of 2007, it was again too dry for Alexander to sample. Then, in early 2008, it re-closed, and during a deluge on June 8, 2008, it became even more plugged with debris.

Eventually, in October and November 2008, the SNA cleared out Goliath's natural entrance using Sentence to Service personnel, people who can work off their jail sentences by performing public works. In the two and a half years since Alexander first submitted his permit application, he has been unable to enter the SNA portion of Goliath's Cave during a time when the water levels were adequate for sampling purposes. It is one of the reasons Alexander has appreciated David's Entrance. In Ackerman's portion of the cave, he has been able to install his sensors, get his water samples, and carry out hydrogeologic research. One of Alexander's sensors, mounted in David's Entrance, recorded a water rise of thirty-seven feet into Ackerman's drilled entrance during the June 8 flood, confirming that in periods of high water the cave is very, very dangerous.

Daniel Doctor, now a geologist with the United States Geological Survey, appreciates the complexity of the current ownership and management of Goliath's Cave. He would never have drilled an entrance into the cave. But it is indicative of his ambivalence about David's Entrance that he hopes, someday, to use the new entrance to enter and explore Goliath's Cave. And true to Ackerman's management of his side of Goliath's Cave, he is more than willing to let Doctor enter the cave, providing he is certain Doctor has the caving expertise and experience to do so. But a simple phone conversation will determine Doctor's level of expertise, not a permit application process.

Doctor hopes that Ackerman's acquisition of part of Goliath's Cave will set a precedent for an informed discussion, or maybe even new legislation that governs the way shared private-public ownership of America's underground natural resources can move forward. For now, he knows, Goliath's Cave is a kind of test case in which the DNR/SNA's need to preserve the site is weighed against the public's right to use it. And what happens when a private citizen like John Ackerman comes along and, through the use of his own resources and expertise, acquires part of a natural resource? What kinds of rights does he have to use it? As joint owners with a divided interest, the DNR/SNA and Ackerman share a space where air and water circulate freely, but people cannot.

For Ackerman's part, he will allow anyone from the DNR to use David's Entrance, providing they are qualified cavers. To date, no one from the DNR has taken him up on his offer. In fact, there seems to be a kind of informal understanding within the DNR that no one in the organization will enter Goliath's Cave through David's Entrance. Neither, as far as Ackerman can tell, will they enter his section of the cave through their own wild entrance. He knows there are those in the DNR who would be very interested in seeing the cave that extends below Venita Sikkink's farm, in seeing the Rubicon passage and the dramatic waterfall near its end. The section of cave beneath David's Entrance seems to be some kind of invisible boundary the interested cavers from the Minnesota Department of Natural Resources will not cross. Perhaps such entry would be seen as a betrayal of the SNA ethic, just as Ackerman's drilling into the cave they controlled but didn't own felt like a betrayal of their management principals.

It is some kind of bizarre modern-day feud. There are those who would love to see his side of the cave, just as he would love to see the SNA portion of the cave. But the SNA staff refuse to enter his side of the cave, and they refuse to allow him entry into their side of the cave, at least without a permit to do valid scientific research.

* * *

This far down, the Rubicon becomes more difficult to traverse. In places, Ackerman and Kraus have to carefully climb down to the streambed or up along the walls. In other parts, the walls become narrow enough so they place their feet on the opposite wall and step sideways along the passage, their gloved hands protecting them against the sharp edges. The ceiling continues to rise.

Everyone agrees there needs to be some kind of control over the entry to Goliath's Cave. Ackerman, like the SNA with the wild entrance, keeps David's Entrance locked. Though there are significantly different requirements between entering the SNA side of Goliath's and the Karst Preserve side, there are still requirements. To enter this cave, any cave, really, is dangerous business.

Consider, for instance, the teens who died entering the man-made caves in St. Paul, the same year John Ackerman purchased his rights to over half of Goliath's Cave. When Ackerman was young, the sandstone mines of St. Paul were among the first caves he entered. But back then they were open and relatively safe. Now they have been made into death traps. And the tragedy that befell the five teens in April 2004 happened precisely because those kids did not know what they were climbing into. They did not know the chambers were filled with dangerous carbon monoxide gas. And they had not lived long enough, or studied cave science or done enough recreational caving, to know underground spaces can hold danger no one can anticipate. It is why recreational caving is one of the most dangerous sports in the world and cave diving is *the* most dangerous.

The deaths of those three teenagers remind both Ackerman and the SNA why entrance into caves, all caves, should be controlled, by either the government or the private citizens who own them.

Down near the end of the Rubicon, the beautiful, long waterfall cascades over the edge of a cliff into a wide pool.

Beyond that streambed, the cave widens out and the ceiling comes down near the floor. Moving any farther down this passage requires a wet suit, endurance, and nerve. But today, Ackerman and Kraus will not have to enter that low streambed. On Ackerman's last visit, he discovered a dry upper-level passage, down near the waterfall. And now, finally, after their long hike down almost two thousand feet of cave, Ackerman and Kraus rise into the narrow passage.

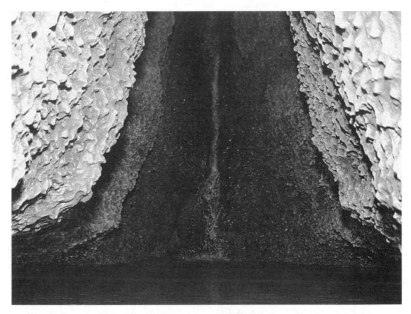

Waterfall at the end of the Rubicon passage, Goliath's Cave. Courtesy John Ackerman

The last time they were here, they moved through almost a quarter mile of new dry cave until they believed they were approximately a hundred feet from Canfield Creek and a major new section of cave. Now they traverse it with the gear that will enable them to explore even farther.

Ackerman, Calvin Alexander, Dave Gerboth, Clay Kraus, Warren Netherton, Daniel Doctor, Mark White, Ellen Fuge, Dawn Ryan, Jim Magnusson, Ron Spong, John Lovaas, Bob Djupstrom, and many, many others recognize that in Goliath's Cave there is controversy, drama, a final frontier of Minnesota that must be preserved and explored. Like other wild caves throughout the state, it is a finite resource and a rare part of the world where, in some instances, man has never before traversed.

Ackerman wants to move through it, carefully and with respect. Today his Karst Preserve holds the keys to six major sections of wild caves, in Minnesota and in Iowa. Cave conservation is one of his stated primary objectives, as are exploration and discovery. To that end, he has opened up more miles of cave through his man-made entrances than has any other private citizen.

Warren Netherton, Mark White, Ellen Fuge, and others have an entirely different perspective, but one that actually begins in the same place as John Ackerman's. These professionals feel that when the cave's wild entrance chokes, or a sump fills with water and no one can enter it, that is the nature of a wild cave. And it must be respected and kept wild. To drill an artificial entrance or open narrow passages with explosives destroys the cave's pristine nature.

And while there has been much tension, conflict, and on

occasion anger between these opposing views, there is enough ambiguity in both to allow for begrudging mutual respect. In a November 2008 phone call, Mark White stated that he admired what Ackerman has been able to do over the years. And John Ackerman appreciates what White and Netherton have done to create a first-class park operation and caving experience through the DNR's Forestville/Mystery Cave State Park.

Both believe the others serve some greater good, something larger than their own self-interests.

Now Ackerman finds the last twenty-foot conduit of narrow passage that will take him to a ledge overlooking a long drop to the streambed below. It is the last dangerous crawl before coming to the ledge that overlooks a deep-set pool of water. This tube is big and round enough to climb into. And its walls have been scoured by water, so its edges are smooth. But the bottom of the tube actually falls away into an eight- to-ten-foot crevasse. The cave walls narrow as they fall away from the tube's bottom and descend to a thin crack.

Ackerman is as far back as anyone has ever been in Goliath's Cave. If he slipped and became wedged into the disappearing floor, he could be stuck there for a very long time, possibly forever. What cavers are capable of coming to this far location to conduct a rescue? And how could a rescue, in such tight spaces, surrounded by tons of impenetrable rock, be conducted? Perhaps this is part of why Kraus lets Ackerman move forward alone.

He crawls, carefully, through the narrow passage, belly to the open floor, bringing with him his drill, bolt, hanger, and finally the cable ladder. At the end, he gets down on the ledge and he can feel the familiar spike in his pulse. Over the ledge, he peers down and sees water, maybe twenty, thirty feet below. It looks like a shallow pool between a narrow constriction of rock. The walls appear to widen back out as they reach down to water.

Ackerman uses his drill to make a hole for the heavy bolt and hanger. He hammers the bolt home and places the hanger on it, testing to make sure it is fastened and secure. Then he places the top end of the ladder over the hanger and lets it drop. It falls between the narrowing walls. There is still room to squeeze between them, but he wonders how far the ladder reaches.

He carefully steps over the edge, holding onto the cable's flexible rungs. He tests the tether as he places more weight on it, leaning against the wall as he eases down onto the first few rungs. It is not an easy thing to accomplish, but this far into Goliath, maybe on the verge of a major discovery, Ackerman is very happy. After all the effort it has taken to reach this place, and all the scrabbling, climbing, bending, and crawling, Ackerman grins.

He lets himself down the ladder slowly, carefully. He works his way down fifteen feet to where the crevice narrows. He slides his body down the contracting walls, and then he discovers what he feared. The walls widen, and the rest of the ladder dangles in the open space down into the water. If he continues working through the narrow crack, he will eventually need to drop down into the pool. And if the ladder is hanging there, without a nearby wall to use as leverage or support, it is going to be difficult to climb back up. But the idea that he could be stuck here, trapped with no possible exit, doesn't really occur to him. Or rather it occurs to him but is heavily outweighed by his desire to see what is down there.

He drops into the water.

"I could tell I had rejoined the lower stream passage," he writes of his experience. "I could look down the stream passage one direction and see that it was sumped. But the other direction, downstream, appeared to have some air space way up ahead. Maybe an inch or two. Since I was not in a wetsuit I did not lay down in the water and go for it. Besides, I was really concerned that I had done something stupid and would need every ounce of energy to get back up this bellied out room and up the tight crevice."

And indeed he does.

After sizing up this opening in the farthest reaches of Goliath's Cave, he returns to the ladder and considers how to climb out. He manages to get up onto the free-hanging rungs, one at a time. He pulls himself up until he can use his body against the walls, gaining enough leverage to rise through the tight constriction of overhead rock. It is a grueling effort, but what other choice is there? Finally, he reaches the ledge and after a moment's rest crawls back—belly to the open floor—through the narrow tunnel conduit.

Ackerman is frustrated. He surmises he may have been less than a hundred feet from the big system he suspects stretches on for a very long time. But he is thankful to be alive.

And almost with his next breath, Ackerman considers new solutions to the puzzle of reaching the elusive ends of Goliath's Cave.

NOTES

General sources consulted for each chapter are provided below, as
are the references for specific quoted material. The research for this
book also involved interviewing the individuals whose stories I tell;
their names are listed in the Acknowledgments.

Abbreviations

CGBV files, SNA
Cherry Grove Blind Valley files, Section of Wildlife, Scientific and
Natural Areas Program, Division of Fish and Wildlife, Minnesota
Department of Natural Resources, St. Paul

MSM
Minnesota Speleology Monthly

MSS
Minnesota Speleological Society

SPFD
St. Paul Fire Department

SPPP
St. Paul Pioneer Press

ST
Star Tribune (Minneapolis)

1 Doorway to the Odessa

Cave trip journal notes from John Ackerman, "The Granger Project: 2000–2001" (2001), copy in author's possession.

p. 12-13, *karst geology*: Constance Jefferson Sansome, *Minnesota Underfoot: A Field Guide to Minnesota's Geology* (St. Paul, MN: Voyageur Press, 1983).

2 Gunpowder

On the discovery of gunpowder, see Mara H. Gottfried, "Gunpowder unearthed from cave on West Side; Bomb squad will destroy '50s material," *SPPP*, Mar. 24, 2004, 8B; Heron Marquez Estrada, "Caves: Good for storing beer, cheese, gunpowder," *SPPP*, Mar. 24, 2004, 3B; and Matt McKinney, "Gunpowder found in St. Paul cave," *ST*, Mar. 23, 2004, B2. For background on Yoerg Brewery caves, see Heron Marquez Estrada, "Underground attractions: Thrill-seeking urban explorers take pride in scouting out forbidden sites," *SPPP*, Sept. 18, 2005, 1B.

p. 30-31, *sandstone geology*: Sansome, *Minnesota Underfoot*.

3 Escape

Ackerman, "The Granger Project."

4 The Authorities

Articles cited for chapter 2, above.

p. 55, *Tracey Baker quote*: Estrada, "Caves: Good for storing beer."

p. 56, *Paul Schnell quote*: Gottfried, "Gunpowder unearthed."

5 After School

Greg Brick, who has explored and written about Minnesota's urban caves, says the five teens entered the east entrance of what some refer to as Fandell's Cave. The drawing on p. 78 was made for the St. Paul Public Works Department by the architectural engineering firm TKDA in 1962. Because the survivors were not available for interviews, I compiled the story from multiple press accounts, listed here by date and source:

Apr. 28, 2004: Mara H. Gottfried and Bill Gardner, "3 teenagers die in St. Paul cave," *SPPP*, 1A; Marie McCain, "Threat can change in cave from day to day," *SPPP*, 10A; "Teens apparently suffocated in cave," *ST*, A1; Matt McKinney, "Efforts to fill caves may have increased danger," *ST*, A11; Patrick Howe, "Three teens die exploring Minn. caves," *Associated Press*; "Three teens die of carbon monoxide in Minnesota cave," *CNN*.

Apr. 29, 2004, *SPPP:* Bill Gardner, "City grieves deaths, vows to close caves," 1A; Mara H. Gottfried, "Rescuers battled time, poisonous gas and terrain," 1A; Allen Powell II and Laura Yuen, "Families, friends tell teens' stories," 10A; Phillip Pina, "For decades, caves have had their fans," 11A; Ruben Rosario, "Despite danger, caves' allure endures," 12A; "Caves attract, but their dangers are far too real," 14A.

Apr. 29, 2004, *ST:* Curt Brown, "A fatal temptation," A1; Jill Burcum and Lourdes Medrano Leslie, "A class clown, a free spirit, a hockey player: Family, friends mourn three teens," A1; Curt Brown, "'You wonder if they'll ever learn,'" A12; Allie Shah and Bill McAuliffe, "Some study the caves, others party," A16.

Apr. 29, 2004: "Parents in Dark on Cave Safety," *CBS*.

Apr. 30, 2004: Jill Burcum, "Cave survivor's recovery amazes doctors," *ST*, B3; John Gessner, "School mourns teens who lost lives in cave," *Thisweek Online*.

On the cave deaths in 1992, see Wayne Wangstand, "17-year-old friends inseparable even in death," *SPPP*, Sept. 28, 1992, 1A; Theresa Monsour, "Cave entrances blocked after 2 deaths, but effort unlikely to deter many," *SPPP*, Sept. 29, 1992, 1B; Conrad deFiebre, "Keeping people out of caves proves to be daunting task," *ST*, Sept. 29, 1992, A1.

p. 60-61, *enumeration of caves and "Most mines"*: CNA Consulting Engineers, "Assessment of Saint Peter Sandstone Mines—Wabasha Street to Lilydale (Prepared for: City of Saint Paul)—Executive Summary, January 2005," copy in author's possession.

p. 64-65, *efforts to fill caves*: McKinney, "Efforts to fill in caves."

p. 65, *Alexander quote*: *ST*, Apr. 28, 2004, A11.

p. 67, *Department of Agriculture building*: The Ramsey County Property Records and Revenue departments now occupy this building.

p. 68, *fires were reported in some of the caves*: CNA Consulting Engineers, "Assessment of Saint Peter Sandstone Mines."

p. 69, *"Refuse fire"*: Incident Report 04—0403661, Fire Investigations, SPFD.

p. 69, *"Smoke coming"*: Incident Report 04—0402661, Fire Investigations, SPFD.

p. 69, *"Smoke odor"*: Incident Report 04—0403727, Fire Investigations, SPFD.

p. 70, *"Caves behind"*: Incident Report 04—0404003, Fire Investigations, SPFD.

p. 70, *"Light smoke"*: Incident Report 04—0404217, Fire Investigations, SPFD.

p. 70, OSHA *standards*: OSHA Fact Sheet: Carbon Monoxide Poisoning, 2002, http://www.osha.gov/OshDoc/data_General_Facts/carbonmonoxide-factsheet.pdf, accessed Dec. 6, 2008.

6 Misfortune

Articles cited for chapter 5, above.

p. 76–77, *Squad 228 police report*: St. Paul Police Department Supplemental Offense / Incident Report, Complaint Number 04082085, 04/27/2004, 15:48:00, St. Paul Police Department.

7 Rescue and Recovery

Articles cited for chapter 5, above. Also, Jackie Crosby and Curt Brown, "St. Paul will seal deadly caves," *ST*, Jan. 26, 2005, B1; "St. Paul strategies: Cave dangers require more risk management,"*SPPP*, Jan. 27, 2005, 10B; Curt Brown, Howie Padilla, "A year after trio died, no answer on caves: St. Paul needs funds to permanently seal entrances," *ST*, Apr. 27, 2005, A1; Tim Nelson, "City to study closing caves," *SPPP*, June 3, 2004, 1B.

8 Aftermath
Articles cited for chapters 5 and 7, above.

9 Discovery
Ron Spong, "Early Spelean History of the Caves of Jessies Grove," 16-page manuscript (2006), copy in author's possession. The map on p. 112 is from *MSM* 16 (Aug. 1984): 126.

p. 105-6, *After a long day's work mapping*: The mapping study was a joint project of the University of Minnesota and the Minnesota Geological Survey, funded by the Legislative Commission on Minnesota Resources.

10 The Unnamed Cave
Issues of *Minnesota Speleology Monthly* cited in the text. The map on p. 126 is from *MSM* 18 (Mar. 1986): 46–47.

p. 122, *"In my mind a primary long term goal"*: Jim Magnusson, "The President's Corner," *MSM* 16 (Aug. 1984): 118, copy in author's possession.

p. 123, *Nearby Mystery Cave*: Mystery Cave was acquired by the State of Minnesota in 1988, when it became part of Forestville/ Mystery Cave State Park.

p. 136, *"In February Dave Madsen"*: Jim Magnusson, "The President's Corner," *MSM* 17 (Feb. 1985): 15, copy in author's possession.

11 Opening Goliath
Issues of *Minnesota Speleology Monthly* cited in the text.

p. 139, *"trickling underground stream"*: Jim Magnusson, "Cave Prospecting Update; Oct. 7, 1984," *MSM* 17 (Mar. 1985): 32, copy in author's possession.

p. 140, *On Sunday, February 17*: Jim Magnusson, "Project Update, Goliath's Cave; Feb. 17, 1985," *MSM* 17 (May 1985): 51, copy in author's possession.

p. 140, *"we really had no idea"*: Magnusson, "Project Update . . . Feb. 17, 1985," 51.

p. 141, *"The passage continued"*: Magnusson, "Project Update . . . Feb. 17, 1985," 51.

p. 146, *"A sharp left"*: Magnusson, "Project Update . . . Feb. 17, 1985," 52

p. 153, *"We pushed and explored"*: Dave Gerboth, Goliath Cave Trip Journal entry, Jan. 18, 1986.

p. 154, *"The ulterior motive"*: Jim Magnusson, "The President's Corner," MSM 18 (May 1986): 69, copy in author's possession.

12 Sinkholes, Sumps, and Gas-powered Pumps
Jim Magnusson, "Project Update, Goliath's Cave; May 2–4, 1986," MSM 18 (June 1986): 81–85, copy in author's possession.

13 Grinding Goliath into Gravel
p. 173, *"We are not taking a position"*: Larry Nelson, Minnesota DNR, to Norman Craig, Fillmore County Zoning Administrator, Dec. 10, 1998, copy in author's possession.

p. 175, *"Frankly, I would prefer"*: E-mail from Calvin Alexander to Glen and Karla Hisey, Dec. 30, 1998, copy in author's possession.

p. 176, *a detailed e-mail*: Calvin Alexander to Bob Djupstrom, Jan. 28, 1999, copy in author's possession.

p. 177, *"Goliath Cave" warning*: Minnesota Department of Natural Resources, *A Guide to Minnesota's Scientific and Natural Areas*, "43. Goliath Cave" (Apr. 1999): 84.

p. 178, *"This is the first time"*: Calvin Alexander to DNR Commissioner Allen Garber, Oct. 20, 1999, copy in author's possession.

p. 181–82, *Commissioner Garber answers*: DNR Commissioner Allen Garber to Professor Calvin Alexander, Nov. 16, 1999, copy in author's possession.

14 The Meeting
MSS Monthly Meeting, minutes taken by Dave Gerboth, July 11, 2001.

15 Drilling

For Ackerman's own account of setting up the Karst Preserve, see *National Speleological Society News,* Apr. 2001, available at http://www.karstpreserve.com/nssarticle.html.

p. 200-201, State of Minnesota, Department of Natural Resources, Division of Fish and Wildlife, Section of Wildlife, Scientific and Natural Areas Program, Special Permit Number 2000-2R, Cherry Grove Blind Valley SNA (Feb. 10, 2000), CGBV files, SNA.

p. 201, *only other permit granted*: Special Permit Number 2000—18R (June 9, 2000), CGBV files, SNA.

p. 210-11, *Alexander sent an e-mail*: E-mail from Calvin Alexander to Jeff Green, DNR Hydrologist, Oct. 11, 2004, copy in author's possession.

p. 211-12, *Ackerman letter*: John Ackerman to Bob Djupstrom, SNA, Oct. 14, 2004, copy in author's possession.

16 David's Entrance

p. 217-18, *Djupstrom . . . makes a record of the call*: Bob Djupstrom, note to file, Nov. 18, 2004, CGBV files, SNA.

p. 219, *unsigned note in the file*: Note to file, Dec. 1, 2004, CGBV files, SNA.

p. 219-20, *Djupstrom and White discuss*: Note to file, Dec. 1, 2004, CGBV files, SNA.

p. 220-21, *Djupstrom's response to his . . . letter:* Bob Djupstrom to John Ackerman, Dec. 29, 2004, CGBV files, SNA.

17 Sump Diving

Lisa Brainard, "'Iconoclast' Ackerman continues cave discoveries; makes national magazine's 'Best of Adventure List,'" and John Ackerman, "Ackerman Shares First Hand Account of Cave Diving," both in *Bluff Country Reader,* Dec. 2005, available at www.karstpreserve.com.

18 The Other Side
Articles cited for chapter 17, above.

19 Exploration, Survey, and Return
Articles cited for chapter 17, above.

20 Beyond the Rubicon
Articles cited for chapter 17, above.

p. 272, *Ryan and Lovaas permit:* Special Permit Number 2006-6R, Cherry Grove Blind Valley SNA (Apr. 21, 2006), CGBV files, SNA.

p. 272, *Alexander and Green permit:* Scientific and Natural Areas Program, Special Permit Number 2007-7R (Mar. 13, 2007), CGBV files, SNA.

p. 280, *"I could tell I had rejoined"*: John Ackerman, e-mail to the MSS list, Goliath's Update, Oct. 13, 2008, copy in author's possession.

ACKNOWLEDGMENTS

As this book was prepared for publication, John Ackerman announced two further cave discoveries. In Tyson Spring Cave, part of the Minnesota Karst Preserve, he found the skull of a saber-toothed tiger and bones from a stag moose, extinct animals whose known ranges had never included Minnesota; the find is causing paleontologists to revise their accounts of ancient life in the region. And while investigating a new sinkhole opened near Granger, Minnesota, by the deluge of June 8, 2008, he found what he has dubbed the Holy Grail Cave system, which is already one of the largest cave systems in the state and perhaps, finally, the entry into the Odessa Spring system for which John has searched so many years.

Like my first nonfiction book, *Lost in the Wild, Opening Goliath* is filled with the stories of all sorts of people who made its writing possible.

Thanks to Kathleen Weflen, Gustave Axelson, Mary Hoff, and others at the *Minnesota Conservation Volunteer*. This book's genesis was "Adventure Underground," an article I wrote for the *Volunteer* (July/Aug. 2005). Research for that article introduced me to the frightening otherworldly drama of caving and the remarkable people who do it.

John Ackerman was open, forthright, and willing to share his journal entries, articles, photos, and whatever else I needed to write this book. In 2004, he guided my son Noah, the filmmaker, and me on a tour of his Spring Valley Caverns. Then in 2008 he took us on an overland and underground tour of the Karst Preserve portion of Goliath's Cave, patiently sat through many interviews, and answered numerous follow-up questions.

Every nonprofit organization should have a keeper of the books, oral historian, and compulsive chronicler like the Minnesota Speleological Survey's Dave Gerboth. He patiently endured numerous interviews and explained all kinds of geologic and general cave information to someone who knew almost nothing about either. Whenever I had questions about times, dates, or what happened when, whenever I needed to find old maps, historical accounts of cave entries, details about cave lengths, or just about anything else, Dave Gerboth knew the answers or where to find them.

I first contacted Calvin Alexander when he was quoted in a newspaper article about the St. Paul sandstone mines. But it wasn't the first time I saw his name associated with all kinds of caving and geologic activity in Minnesota and elsewhere. Calvin, too, sat through plenty of interviews and read through several chapters and was extremely helpful in editing some of this book's text for accuracy. He identified photos and put me in touch with people on all sides of the Goliath's Cave controversy. Time and again, I was struck by his diplomacy and ability to see all sides of any caving issue. The University of Minnesota and the state itself are lucky to be represented by him.

When I finally tracked down Karl Schaak, he willingly shared his story and photos of finding gunpowder in the St. Paul sandstone mines. His subsequent reading of those two chapters was both appreciated and helpful.

The chapters of the book that follow the tragic course the five teens took into Fandell's Cave were compiled almost entirely from press accounts appearing in both local and national publications. Understandably, Jay Boucher, one of two survivors still in Minnesota, did not want to speak about that day. And Justin Jensen, the only other survivor, could not be located. Two of their friends helped fill in some details. But sifting through all the news accounts and the quotes from the survivors and others raised some questions about what actually happened. I tried to address these, and I hope the effort was successful.

Several firefighters who participated in the rescue and recovery effort were particularly helpful in detailing what occurred that day, including Martin Ludden, Geno Flores, Bill Lee, Mike Scheller, and Mike Selander, among others. The chapter on the rescue and recovery could not have been written without their full cooperation and assistance.

Greg Brick, PhD, well-known cave historian, member of St. Paul Mayor Randy Kelly's 2004 cave consultation committee, and MSS member since 1988, provided background and a map of the area the teens entered. Greg also reviewed a draft of the final manuscript and made suggestions for improvements. His assistance and knowledgeable expertise are greatly appreciated. Ron Spong provided some of the first maps of the entryway to Goliath's and gave me an excellent introduction to the cave's early history and first accounts of discovery and exploration. A very busy Jim Magnusson, the cave's first consistent explorer and probably discoverer of many of the cave's passages, exchanged a few e-mails and brief phone calls with me to verify some details. While he was unable to sit down for a full interview, he gave me access to his thorough trip reports of the early discovery and exploration of Goliath's Cave throughout the mid-1980s. He was an excellent chronicler of many excursions into Goliath's Cave and of the work he and fellow cavers did to dig a new entrance. Dave Madsen reviewed the opening chapter of their entry into Goliath's Cave and verified its accuracy. In a few e-mails, phone calls, and one long interview, John Preston related the particulars of his and John Ackerman's discovery, entry, and exploration of Goliath's new Iconoclast Section, and he has also let us use some of his fine photographic work, including the book's cover photo. And thanks to cave expert Art Palmer, who provided several stunning photographs of Goliath's Cave, most notably the Goliath formation for which the cave is named.

A crowd of DNR people were particularly helpful in telling me how the acquisition of Goliath's Cave evolved and finally transpired and in relating some of the politics involved with subsequent management of the site. Mark White, Warren Netherton, Jeff Green, Larry Nelson, Don Nelson, Lee Markell, and others at the DNR were informative and helpful.

Peggy Booth, current supervisor of the Scientific and Natural Areas Program (SNA), was welcoming and willing to share numerous details about the program. She granted full access to files on the Cherry Grove Blind Valley SNA (Goliath's Cave). And during one long afternoon when my oldest son Nick did some research in the SNA offices, she guided him to the right sources and helped make copies of the files he needed. Peggy reviewed the manuscript and offered several excellent and much appreciated suggestions for improvement. Ellen Fuge also provided insight into the SNA's perspective about management of these pristine areas. And Bob Djupstrom, former supervisor of the SNA and the one who spearheaded the effort to acquire Goliath's Cave as part of the SNA program, shared his perspective on the SNA's acquisition of the property. Through one long interview and several follow-up inquiries, he related his memory of the 2001 meeting with the MSS, and once the chapter was finalized he reviewed it for accuracy. Particular thanks to Assistant Professor Jeffrey Dorale, University of Iowa, Department of Geoscience, who reviewed the manuscript and offered many suggestions to improve the book's discussions of geology and cave science.

While I wrote this book, no one else worked harder, longer, or in more detail on it than Ann Regan, editor in chief at the Minnesota Historical Society Press/Borealis Books. She is a tough editor who can applaud a nail-biting scene ("In-bloody-credible. Unbe-dang-lievable. Whew!") and tease an author who loses track of the depth of the entry drilled into a cave ("Was 75 feet, then 80, now 85? This is the way my *brother* tells stories!").

And finally, many thanks to my family and friends. My family heard countless stories about my interviews during the writing of this book; without their support and occasional readings, *Opening Goliath* would not be in your hands today. Particular thanks to my wife, Anna McCourt, who read several of these chapters after they were written and gave me invaluable feedback, and to my son Nick, who helped me research the book, and to my son Noah, who helped me interview John Ackerman and whose video vignettes of Goliath's Cave are posted on www.caryjgriffith.com.

To honor Minnesota's remarkable cavers, six percent of the author's proceeds from this book will be donated to the Minnesota Speleological Survey, to the Karst Preserve, and to Minnesota's Scientific and Natural Areas program, to be divided equally. Their combined efforts have provided us with a wealth of knowledge about Minnesota's caving resources and an excellent conservation and preservation structure on which to build.